A Guide To Assimilation in the Local Church

Improving Your Church's Retention Capacity

By

Owen Facey D. Min

This book is a work of fiction. Places, events, and situations in this story are purely fictional. Any resemblance to actual persons, living or dead, is coincidental.

© 2002 by Owen Facey. All rights reserved.

No part of this book may be reproduced, stored in a retrieval system, or transmitted by any means, electronic, mechanical, photocopying, recording, or otherwise, without written permission from the author.

ISBN: 1-4033-3773-X (e-book)
ISBN: 1-4033-3774-8 (Paperback)

Library of Congress Control Number: 2002106680

This book is printed on acid free paper.

Printed in the United States of America
Bloomington, IN

1stBooks - rev. 12/03/02

TABLE OF CONTENTS

INTRODUCTION vii

CHAPTER 1 DEFINING ASSIMILATION 2

    Assimilation - What is it? 4
    Key Concepts 13
    For Reflection and Action 14

CHAPTER 2 PRE-EVANGELISTIC EVENTS AND ASSIMILATION 17

    What are Pre - Evangelistic Events? 19
    Helpful Steps for Doing Effective Pre-evangelistic Events 24
    Community Networking and Involvement 24
    Work as the Arena for Ministry 32
    Key Concepts 38
    For Reflection and Action 39

CHAPTER 3 PROVIDING RAILS AND ASSIMILATION 42

    Rails - What are They? 44
    Key Concepts 52
    For Reflection and Action 53

CHAPTER 4 ASSIMILATION AND FIRST IMPRESSION MINISTRIES 55

First Impression Ministries.............................. 58
Key Concepts... 64
For Reflection and Action 66

CHAPTER 5 ASSIMILATION AND CHURCH IDENTITY 68

Moving from a Casual Attender to a Part of the Body of Christ 72
Developing a Clear Vision for Your Church.......... 76
Key Concepts... 84
For Reflection and Action 85

CHAPTER 6 FULLY ASSIMILATED-FINDING MY PLACE IN MINISTRY 87

My Ministry Profile.. 90
Key Concepts... 95
For Reflection and Action 96

CHAPTER 7 ASSIMILATION AND YOUR BACKDOOR 98

Back Door Ministries 104
Compassionate Ministries 109
Follow-up Ministries 112
Key Concepts... 115
For Reflection and Action 116

CHAPTER 8 STARTING THE PROCESS OF ASSIMILATION IN YOUR CHURCH................... 119

Community Assessment 123
Developing a Clear Strategy 126
Key Concepts 131
For Reflection and Action 132

CHAPTER 9 ASSIMILATION AND THE TECHNOLOGICAL REVOLUTION 134
Over View of Some Church Management Software 137
Recommended Customization 143
Calculating Assimilation 145
Key Concepts 148
For Reflection and Action 149

CONCLUSION 150
APPENDIX 154
WORKS CITED 174

INTRODUCTION

The writer of the book of Proverbs says "the fruit of the righteous is a tree of life, and he who wins souls is wise" (Prov. 11:30). This is an important admonition for Christians in a time when the Church seems to be marginalized from the main stream in society. Many Christians find it embarrassing to share their faith, because it is not the "cool" thing to do. Many churches have adopted a survival mode of operation. They are just merely maintaining what they have, without the will or insight to do more. But the question that must be asked is this. Is a survival mode of operation enough for the Church; especially when God has called it to reach a lost world? It cannot be enough. History has made that clear. The Church must face the challenge of each age and re-appropriate the message of the gospel and boldly declare it.

Throughout history the Christian Church has proven to be one of the most adaptable and resilient movements. It is adaptable because of the power and nature of the message it proclaims. This message is about God sending his son Jesus Christ to earth as a visible demonstration of God himself in order to reconcile humanity back to himself. The adaptability of the Church, however, has sometimes resulted in the confusion of its message. The confusion of the central message of God sending his son to reconcile human beings to himself has further led to the Church becoming delinquent about its central task of reaching the lost. So while the Church has proven to be adaptable over the centuries, it has not always been forthright and effective about the task of evangelizing the lost.

The key responsibility that each church has is to both be a student of the culture in which it resides and the scriptures. In doing this each church should be able to develop new and more effective methods of sharing Christ. I believe this is what the bible means when it says "those who win souls are wise." This assimilation guide outlines a simple path that, if taken seriously, should help churches become more culturally relevant and biblically authentic in reaching, nurturing and releasing people to build God's kingdom.

This guide is divided into nine sections. The format that is used is to employ the use of an illustrative story to start each chapter. The story illustrates the principles of assimilation. The chapters flesh out the principles. At the end of each chapter is a section entitled "For Reflection and Action." The goal of this section is to help churches begin an assimilation ministry. It is recommended that this guide be used in a leadership team setting. In this setting the key leaders of the church can pour over the principles and then help to move the congregation to take the necessary steps to start the assimilation process.

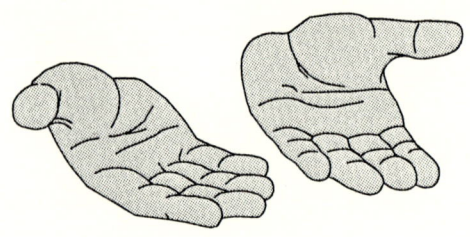

We are encouraged to share the gospel - so give it away!

A Guide to Assimilation in the Local Church

Do we have to move?

CHAPTER 1

DEFINING ASSIMILATION

Do we have to move so soon? This was the question that summed up the frustration of the Welsh family. After all life was going well in the city of Fort Lauderdale where they had lived for the past years. Now Pat and his wife Nancy were enduring the anxiety of moving. Nancy had a comfortable job, working for an accounting firm in down town Fort Lauderdale.

Pat's job was going reasonably well but friction started developing between him and his boss. They were no longer seeing "eye to eye" on important issues that could impact the bottom line of the company. Just as he was contemplating looking for another job an opportunity came up. He was offered a branch managers' position in Orlando. "The banking business is such a "cut-throat" business. When you are offered a position you better take it. You really do not know when the opportunity will come again," Pat said to Nancy.

For many long hours Pat and Nancy wrestled with the decision to move. Finally the decision was made. They moved to the north west side of Orlando. They had just shown up at their new house. The moving truck had also just arrived. The movers were busy unloading the furniture in the Welsh's new house. About that time Tim was just coming home from work, as he drove up he saw the moving truck and thought he would go over to help. Of course this new family was going to be Tim's and Dianne's neighbor.

"Hello," Tim said. "I am your neighbor. My name is Tim. Do you need some help?" "Sure," Pat said. "As you might know these guys are from the moving company. They are being paid to unload this stuff, but if you are available later, we could sure use your help to unpack and arrange furniture." Tim agreed that latter he would be back to help Pat and his wife arrange the furniture.

Assimilation - What is it?

The *Oxford Dictionary* defines assimilation as "absorbing into a system." Robert Bast in his book *Attracting New Members* sees assimilation as having three components: absorption, integration, and incorporation. Assimilation as absorption is to bring into the tradition of a group. Assimilation as integration is to coordinate or blend into a unified whole. Assimilation as incorporation is to unite into one body (1988:132).

The late Sylvia Glenn, former minister of assimilation at the Church of the Crossing Indianapolis Indiana adds four other programmatic components to assimilation. She said that assimilation must be intentional, planned, aggressive and focused (n.d.:3).

These elements are programmatic because they describe the thought process, strategic planning and kind of executive actions that must accompany any effective assimilation ministry.

Reflecting on the above definitions of assimilation would lead one to conclude that assimilation is more than just a one time act, rather it is a process. Assimilation is the process of intentionally binging, including, integrating people into the life of the local church with the goal of equipping and releasing them to serve both the local church and the kingdom of God. It is a process of intentionally brining new people into the body of Christ. It involves including them into the body of Christ, and finally integrating them into the body of Christ. It involves equipping and then releasing them to serve the local church and the kingdom of God. All these stages must be planned and focused.

It is necessary to do a little demythologizing at this point. Many churches tend to think of assimilation as newcomer follow-up. This is to limit the definition and ultimately the practice of assimilation within the local church. Newcomer follow-up implies activities that are done with visitors after they have attended church for the first time. In actuality assimilation starts before a person attends church for the first time. In addition, assimilation is also intricately linked to evangelism.

George Hunter III, in his book *Apostolic Churches*, says that churches that are really on the edge assimilate people before they attend church for the first time (1996:166). If churches will do effective assimilation it is critical that they understand that certain ministry activities must be happening in the community that begin the process of newcomer assimilation. An example of such activities would be Tim reaching out to his new neighbor in physical, hands-on help. This same act of Tim reaching out into the community to help the Welsh's, in some circles, is called pre-evangelism. It really does not matter what it is called, this act connected with the Welsh family at a critical point of need. It initiated them to the love of Christ and his church through Tim.

One of the reasons many churches struggle to assimilate newcomers is because they concentrate too much on follow-up and not initiation. By initiation the reference is being made to intentionally developing ministries in the community that seek to begin the process of connecting new people to the church and to Christ.

Another reason churches struggle with assimilation is that they divorce it from evangelism. Churches cry often that they have a wide proverbial "backdoor." The truth is they have a closed "front door." The only people who visit periodically are immediate family members of the members of the church. Most of these family members are often coming from out of town and are not good assimilation prospects, because of proximity. The point being made here is not that immediate family members do not need Christ and therefore do not qualify as visitors coming through the "front door." Rather family members coming to visit their relatives often find it tasteful to attend the church their relatives attend. Getting out of town relatives to accompany one to church does not take much intentionality.

If a church keeps some sort of records yearly of visitors attending church over the course of the year, without a proper filter system, it could easily conclude that it had a lot of visitors whom it was unable to assimilate. The question then is who were these visitors? If they were out of town family members visiting, the chances of their being assimilated would be unlikely in the first place. Therefore, their not being assimilated does not qualify as having a wide "back door." A wide "back door" exists when legitimate visitors, who are potential prospects for assimilation attend church, but were not connected in anyway. These legitimate prospects do not come without intentionality on the part of the church. Attracting legitimate prospects means church and people must develop a certain mind set that allows them to do certain things.

It is often said that the longer one is a Christian the fewer unchristian friends one tends to have. As sad as this sounds it is true. As the old adage goes "birds of a feather do tend to flock together." Christians like to hang out with Christians. When this happens the necessary relationships with non Christians that need to be in place in order to do effective assimilation is not nurtured. Churches must be intentional in developing ministries that are focused out in the wider community to build relationships with non Christians.

When a church strategically executes ministries that are designed to build relationships with the non

Christians several things happen that will affect the way the church will continue to do ministry. First, the people in the congregation begin to connect with the overall mission of the church, which is to reach the lost (Matt. 28:19-20). Second, individuals in the congregation begin to develop a mentality to cultivate relationships with people who are not Christians. At this point assimilation is moving from programmatic and organizational to a more personal and organic view. When assimilation is organizational and programmatic the congregation waits on the church as a whole to develop an assimilation program to reach non-Christians. With the success or lack of success that some churches tend to have with programs, such organizational assimilation efforts are few and far between.

A word needs to be said here about the relationship between assimilation and evangelism. It is impossible to do assimilation without evangelism. After all a church has to reach those whom it will assimilate. If assimilation is integrating people into the tradition of a church then only people who have not been integrated need to be. These people would have to be people who are new to the church and consequently coming as a result of some evangelism effort. One could conceive of the integrating process in assimilation as discipleship. Discipleship is a step that follows evangelism. The point being made is that assimilation cannot be independent of evangelism. Evangelism reaches the lost and assimilation incorporates and integrates them into the body of Christ. In this sense, if evangelism is not happening then assimilation also does not happen either.

When assimilation is organic peoples' psychic is trained to share Christ at a personal level. They don't have to wait on a church to mobilize them to practice evangelism. Consequently, assimilation becomes a natural process. This should be the goal of all churches to develop a consciousness within Christians to minister naturally instead of programmatically. In Tim's case this was exactly what he was doing. He was not executing a church program. He was doing something that came naturally to him. He was sharing his faith and at the same time starting the assimilation process with the Welsh family.

When the church becomes involved in ministry in the community the community perceives it differently. Sometimes churches are accused of being too institutional and not community oriented enough. Ministries that are geared to build relationships in the community will go a long way in allowing the community to see that the church is community minded. Tim's action would allow a person who is not a Christian to see him first as a nice person trying to help rather than a Christian trying to push a religious agenda.

The purpose of this guide is to lay out in as simple a way as possible a path to help churches become more effective in their assimilation efforts. It is important for churches to understand at the onset that assimilation and evangelism are intricately tied. Assimilation cannot be done without evangelism. And evangelism should not be done without assimilation otherwise the church becomes guilty of still birth.

Key Concepts

Assimilation: It is intentionally connecting new people to Christ and his Church, absorbing integrating and incorporating them into the body of Christ, with the purpose of leading them to maturity such that they are released to serve the local church and the kingdom of God.

Integration: Integration is the process where by people are coordinated and blended into a unified whole. This happens when people are guided to a commitment to Christ and his Church. This wholeness is becoming a part of the body of Christ.

Initiation: Initiation is intentionally developing ministry opportunities that seek to introduce people to Christ and his Church.

Incorporation: It is to unite in or to become one body. The members of a church function as one body when each person is guided to discover his or her ministry profile. In so doing each person is contributing to the overall mission of the church and ultimately God's kingdom.

For Reflection and Action

1. How does your church assimilate new people into its life?

2. What ministries do you currently have that are based in the community that are designed to start the process of new member assimilation?

3. If your church does not have any such ministries what are some possible ministries that could be developed?

Are those Christians?

CHAPTER 2

PRE-EVANGELISTIC EVENTS AND ASSIMILATION

Later that evening Tim and Dianne showed up to help Pat and Nancy unpack and arrange furniture. They worked and chatted into the late hours of the night. During their visit Tim got to find out that Pat and Nancy were under a tremendous amount of stress. In spite of the fact that this move was very good for Pat's career, Nancy was struggling with it. After all her job was just as important. She was very secure in her job. Why could not the decision be made in her interest? Nancy was becoming resentful.

That evening Pat and Nancy talked freely about the stress that they were under. Tim started thinking how could I help? Immediately, Tim remembered, that while he was in church on Sunday he saw an announcement on the church's multimedia projection screen. It was announcing a stress management seminar that would be offered at the church the following weekend. It was free to the public. In fact the congregation was encouraged to invite as many people as possible to the seminar.

"Pat and Nancy," Tim said, "I know that I do not know you much, but from what we have been talking about tonight, it sounds like you both are under a lot of stress. I do not know what you might think of this. But the other day I was in church and I saw an announcement about a stress management seminar that was being offered at the church. It is free of charge. This might be just what you both need. Would you like to go? I could get the details." Pat looked at Nancy. He started to say "no. . . Tim I think we will be . . . ." Just then Nancy piped in "I think it would be a good idea Tim. If you will come with us we would like to try it."

What are Pre - Evangelistic Events?

When a church thinks of assimilation one of the first steps that need to be taken is assessment. The community must be carefully assessed to determine where the pains of the community lie. Also it is necessary to determine what are the crying needs of the community. Typically it is through the addressing of these needs that people will be drawn to Christ. When the needs of the community are identified a church can now develop pre-evangelistic ministries that revolve around the meeting of such needs.

By community the reference is being made to the immediate community in which the church resides. For some churches this might be an entire city, if the city is small. For others it might be a certain geographic portion of the city. At any rate community refers to the immediate area that falls within the sphere of the church's influence.

Pre-evangelistic events are those ministries that are designed to build relationships with people, thereby raising their awareness to the love of God. These ministries can be done in the community or on the church grounds. It is preferable to do pre-evangelistic ministries on the church grounds since such events have the power of breaking down certain defenses and fears that non-Christians might have. Non-Christians often possess certain preconceived ideas about the church. These ideas act as barriers to their attending church. Interestingly, some such ideas that these non-Christians have are fixed to certain historical periods and experiences. Consequently, their opinion of the church might not be current. When they attend a non-threatening event on the church's premises, they get a chance to see that the church is not so bad after all. They might then be inclined to attend again.

If pre-evangelistic events are being done at a location other than the church premises it is important that a focused effort is made to allow the community to know who is sponsoring the event. People should be able to link the event with the church.

A critical element of a church being engaged in pre-evangelistic events is developing a clear structure or process to help people move from attending these events to attending others and ultimately meeting Christ. Some of the ways this can be done is to air moments during the event, where happenings of the church are highlighted. Care should be taken to do this effectively. These moments should not be seen as the typical boring Sunday morning announcements. Drama, video clips and other forms of multimedia avenues should be used to make these highlights memorable.

One word of caution with the communication of these highlights. The announcements should be restricted only to those opportunities that provide the next logical step from the pre -evangelistic events. An example could be the following. If the pre-evangelistic event being done is a divorce seminar, the appropriate announcement that could be made is the starting of a small group that seeks to help people work through the difficulties of a divorce.

Another from of assessment that needs to be done concerns the church itself. The church must be aware of its resources, both financially and people wise. It is unwise to undertake a pre-evangelistic event that the church has no financial resources to underwrite. It is also challenging to provide a ministry in an area where the church has no people resources.

The combination of careful community and church assessments should lead to the development of contextually appropriate pre-evangelistic events. Pre-evangelistic events are often the missing link in many churches' assimilation efforts. A church cannot afford to wait until people attend. It must take Jesus story of the lost sheep recorded in Luke 15 seriously. The church must go and find the lost sheep. This is what pre-evangelistic events do.

There is really no shortage of such events. A few examples could be music festivals, need based small groups, divorce care, rebuilding, stress management, managing your money, marriage enrichment, young offenders programs, seniors' ministries. The list could go on. The important issue is every church must identify the ministries that are most appropriate for its context. Then it must do the hard work of developing follow through ministries. It is futile just to have a pre-evangelistic ministry in isolation from other ministries. A clear strategic progression must be thought out. An example of a progression could be: Divorce care as a pre-evangelistic ministry, then a rebuilding group as the next step, after which a building meaningful relationship group.

The advantage of having these strategic progressions is that people get a chance to build solid relationships with class members and the church. In the process of taking such classes members should meet Christ. When conversion happens in this form discipleship is much easier and more effective because the relationships are already in place.

Helpful Steps for Doing Effective Pre-evangelistic Events

Some important steps are necessary when planning pre-evangelistic events. First, community networking is essential. Second, the congregation must be trained to see work as an arena for ministry. And, third pre-evangelism should not stand on its own. It must be linked to an overall process.

Community Networking and Involvement

The first step in developing any kind of ministry is vision casting. According to Robert Logan and Larry

Short, to build a vision for ministry involvement in the community requires training people to look in certain ways. "The reality is wherever there are human beings, there are human hurts. If we are surrounded with people, if we have our eyes open to our community as we live in it, we will see the ministry opportunities that are all around us" (1994:27). To see ministry opportunities a congregation must become involved in the community. Some of the ways that vision casting for community involvement can be done are through, sermons, teaching times, and partnering with community agencies to address needs.

Community awareness can be accomplished by conducting a series of community information nights. Community leaders can be invited from different agencies to come and share with your congregation what they perceive as being some of the key needs in the community. These leaders should be encouraged to share with the church how they think the church could partner with their agencies in helping to address these needs.

At these awareness evenings the option should be given to members who might want to talk more about, or become involved in ministering in these areas to meet with church leaders at a different time to put together a plan. After these awareness evenings the church should begin a process of discovering those who might possess the gifts and passion for some of the areas addressed.

Several criteria should determine which needs the church would seek to address; the church's vision, its strengths, and intended audience. It is important that the needs the church seeks to address align with the vision, strength of the congregation, and the intended audience. From the list of issues discussed, leaders would take a look at the vision and church resources to see what needs are consistent with both. This is critical since no church will be able to be all things to all people. The members would be encouraged to work in the areas of their strengths. Lyle Schaller observes, "the clearer and the more precise the definition of a congregation's audience, the easier it is to design a strategy to reach and serve that audience" (1994:54).

In order not to attempt to develop too many ministries a limit of two significant long term pre-evangelistic ministries could be attempted to start the process. Other event oriented ministries could also be done yearly. The primary criteria that should determine which two long term, and event oriented ministries would be developed are; the magnitude of the need in the community, the available resources (both people, and finances) in the congregation, and again the vision of the congregation.

Once enough people have been recruited to see a certain ministry develop, training should follow. Leaders in the community would again be brought in to help in the training process. Depending on the peoples' gifted-ness, passion, and availability, leaders should be developed to execute and oversee the various areas of ministries.

Another way that people could be encouraged to become involved in the community is through data gathering. Data could be gathered from the Police Department in respect to crime and drug activities, the Department of Social Services in regards to social and economic ills families experience, and the community safe shelters concerning domestic abuse. People who might posses administrative gifts and the passion to gather and compile data would be enlisted to minister in these areas. The result of this community research should be tabulated and presented to the congregation through teaching and vision casting times. This information should be used to stir up passion in people during sermon times. Once members have received a sense of what the community is like, other need specific, ministries could be developed.

One of the results of encouraging members to get involved in community data gathering is that they will have first hand experience of some of the things that are happening in the community. This process will help to ignite in them a passion for community involvement type ministries. Their passion can in turn stir up passion in other members of the congregation. Also another advantage of members becoming involved in data gathering is that they are moved beyond the walls of the church to the places where the greatest needs are. Usually these are the places that afford the best opportunities to share the gospel.

It might be necessary to say at this point that ministry follows passion. I do not believe in leaders developing ministries and then imposing such ministries on the congregation. The result of such efforts have had many negative effects. Rather leaders "define reality" for members. By defining reality, the reference is to leaders creating a context for ideas and passion to develop within members such that fruitful ministries can follow. Max DePree notes that one of the responsibilities of a leader is to define reality (1989:11). Community awareness helps to define reality for members. Members get a chance to see first hand what the community is like. They begin to see where they can become involved in making a difference.

The benefits of these kinds of community involvement ministries are many. First, the church gets a chance to network with community leaders who might not be Christians. The hope is that, in time, these community leaders will become Christians. Second, the stereotype that churches are not involved in the community would be broken. The church would be visibly attempting to partner with community agencies to address people's needs. These acts would clearly communicate to the community that the church is concerned with more than soul care issues. The church cares about the whole person. Third, people would become more aware of the church and what it is about.

Michael Green comments that one of the reasons Christians are reluctant to become engaged in evangelism is that they have lost a sense of the lostness of souls. This happens because many churches are organized for maintenance rather than growth (1990:398). The reluctance to become involved in evangelism among Christians also happens because many of them tend to isolate themselves from the pains of the community. It is only when Christians begin to feel the pain of the community that the hope of Christ can be offered and evangelism can take place. On several occasions as Jesus traveled through the towns and villages in Judea, he was moved by people's plight. He felt their pain and had compassion on them (Matt. 9:35-38, 14:14, 15:32, Mk. 1:41, 6:34, Lk. 15:20). Much like in the examples of Jesus, when Christians are involved in the community they are moved to compassionate action. Pre-evangelism gets the church involved in the pains of the community which results in compassionate ministries.

Work as the Arena for Ministry

One of the keys in empowering a congregation to do evangelism is to encourage members to use their work places as ministry arenas. According to Robert Slocum "the time has come when ordinary Christians assigned by Christ to the Church Scattered also need a corporate motto: 'the world is your office' when you follow Jesus Christ!"(1990:185) The strength of Slocum's argument lies in who he is. He is a lay person raising the issue that churches too often divide between the world of the church and the world of work. Slocum's concern supports the contention that the workplace must be seen as an arena for ministry.

A part of the strategy to becoming engaged in doing effective assimilation through pre-evangelistic events is to help church members realize that their work place is for ministry. This could be encouraged in sermons, small group times, or just about any time there is a chance to cast a vision. At this point it does not matter what kind of gifts people may possess, they should be encouraged to use their workplaces for ministry. Of course members would have to work with respect to the rules and regulations that govern their work.

Some of the ways that members could use their work places for ministry are the following. First, just by being a friend. From time to time co-workers struggle. If Christians portray themselves as friends then they might be the first ones to whom such struggles are brought. This becomes a time for ministry. J. I. Packer writes "the truth is that real personal evangelism is very costly, just because it demands of us a really personal relationship with the other man. We have to give ourselves in honest friendships to the point at which we are justified in choosing to talk to them about Christ and can speak to them about their own spiritual needs . . . (1966:82).

Second, co-workers might be struggling without necessarily saying anything. A caring Christian might be alert enough to see such a concern and respond. The responses could vary. Maybe a Christian could simply leave an open invitation to talk at a time convenient to both people. Other times Christians might just offer to pray. Sometimes co-workers might be in need of practical things. This is an opportunity for Christians to communicate love through giving.

For Christians to use their workplaces for ministry requires a mental reorientation. Many Christians see their workplaces as only for work. Therefore they are not vigilant enough to see the ministry opportunities that might be happening around them. If Christians are trained to look for avenues of ministry at work then they are more likely to see them when they develop.

People who are actively sharing Christ through pre-evangelism could be encouraged to share public testimonies in the worship services on how God is working in their personal lives. This is part of creating that mental shift by a process of hero making. DePree discussed the importance of hero making in galvanizing a vision. He says every company has tribal stories. These tribal stories need to be told. As these stories are told people catch the vision of what the company is all about (1989:92). Telling tribal stories is a part of creating a mentality that sees the work place as an arena for ministry.

Telling tribal stories is also a part of encouraging members to continue doing the right things. James Kouzes and Barry Posner suggest that leaders must recognize and reward the contributions of employees. They write, "you are not aware that your behavior toward people is based upon your expectations about them . . . treating people in a friendly, pleasant, and positive fashion and being attentive to their needs produce increased performance because of the favorable effect on employee motivation" (1995:243-244).

The point they are making is that when people are recognized for what they do it has a double effect. They are motivated to do more and others looking on might also catch the vision to become involved. This is hero making. It is a central part of encouraging members to use their work places as a ministry arena.

A goal of pre-evangelism is that it helps people see that in spite of the gifts that they might have, their ministry contributes to the whole. Pre- evangelism will help the church see that ministry is about getting dirty. It is about getting involved in real issues and seeking to make a difference. Hopefully, it is by being involved in real concerns, that seekers will begin to ask the obvious question, why do you love me so much? It is at this point that the church now earns the right to share the gospel with them. The reality is because the church was involved in their lives, the church now has a place of trust in seekers minds.

One of the mistakes that Christians often make in their zeal to evangelize, is the tendency to side step people's real pain and seek to address their spiritual condition. In the Romans 12 passage Paul reminds us that the spiritual gifts are for practical purposes, such as helping the needy or showing hospitality. Pre-evangelistic events embody the serving aspect of ministry. Pre-evangelistic events bring people to the door of the kingdom. Pre-evangelistic events or activity is the first step to doing effective assimilation. A church must reach people before it can integrate them. Because Tim's church understood the importance of pre-evangelistic events that are need based it was easy for him to get the Welsh's family involved in something that they desperately needed.

Key Concepts

Pre-evangelistic: Pre-evangelistic events are those ministries that are designed to build relationships with people, thereby rasing their awareness to the love of God.

Community: The community is the precise target group or area that a church is trying to reach.

Divorce Care: This is a series developed by a group out of Wake Forest, North Carolina. It is a ministry of Church Initiative. It is designed to help people deal with and find healing from the pains of Divorce.

Rebuilding: Rebuilding is a group that is built on Bruce Fisher's book *Rebuilding When Your Relationship Ends.* It is designed to help people move a little further in the healing process and ultimately start rebuilding their lives.

Building Meaningful Relationships: Building Meaningful relationship is a group developed by Owen Facey (the author of this guide) that seeks to help people examine the sociological, psychological and spiritual dynamics of relationships. The goal is to help people build stronger relationships through understanding themselves and others.

For Reflection and Action

1. What does your church know about the needs in your community?
2. What are some key agencies or places in your community from which you can gather data?
3. What does you church do best?

4. What unique gifts or resources does your church have that could make a difference in your community?

A Guide to Assimilation in the Local Church

Where are the rails?

CHAPTER 3

PROVIDING RAILS AND ASSIMILATION

The following Saturday Pat, Nancy, Tim and Dianne attended the stress management seminar. The first session covered a little about the human physiology and how it is designed to function. The second session dealt with the physical effects of stress and the psychological effects on relationships. It was in this session the bells started going off for Nancy. For the past few days she had been having continuous headaches. Her stomach was always tightening up. Her nights were long and sleepless. She would get out of bed in the mornings tired.

Pat on the other hand listened attentively. Mid way through the second session, a few beads of tears started running down his cheek. Quietly he reached over and grasped his wife's Nancy's hand, as if to apologize for the stresses he had caused her.

In between sessions Pat and Nancy had a heart to heart talk. The stress management seminar helped Pat to see how insensitive he was to his wife in her time of need. Nancy was over loaded, trying to balance this move with her career dreams. She felt Pat was not understanding her. He was just selfishly pursuing his dreams. That was a watershed point for them. The question that they now faced was what were they going to do about it? This question was the subject of the final session of the stress management seminar.

During the final session Pat leaned over and quietly whispered into Tim's ear. "That guy who is talking, I think I really like him. He seems to know his stuff." "O Dr Keene is a very respected psychologist in this community," Tim said. "In fact he comes to our church." Pat started, "I wonder if . . . Its o. k." Tim looked at him somewhat quizzically, he was about to ask a question but decided to refrain.

Dr. Keene outlined a strategy to overcome stress. Included in that strategy was a twelve weeks class designed to help people identify the stressors in their lives and develop an action plan to overcome stress. Pat had already made the decision that he wanted to attend this session. He now had to talk to Nancy to see if she was interested.

Rails - What are They?

I know of a church which started a day care ministry some time ago. At that time the church was growing steadily and the board and pastor thought that a day care ministry was a good thing to do. It has now been over twenty years. The day care ministry continues to thrive and the church is in decline. In fact both the day care and the church operate as separate entities. In spite of the fact that the day care ministry has a very good reputation in the city, the church is unable to capitalize on that reputation. Strategically the day care is not linked to the church. Consequently it is difficult to bridge people from the day care to the church.

The Chesta Peak Community church provides us with another example of how a church can develop adequate rails that guide a person from the community of unbelievers to the community of believers. This church had a clear vision to minister effectively to the community. It had a number of need based small groups, empowerment type ministries, and it was always active in community issues. Through such involvements this church had developed a solid network with the various service agencies in the city. One of the advantages of having firm partnerships with community agencies was that the Chesta Peak Community church was the first Church with which the Department of Social Services communicated when they saw a need to develop an empowerment type program for troubled youth in the city.

Out of the initial communication with the Department of Social Services, the Chesta Peak Community Church developed the "Fresh Start" Program. This was a program designed to take high risk youth and provide them with some form of work. In the process these youth developed some work skills, learn some life skills and over time corrected their high risk behavior patterns.

The church played a vital role in establishing this ministry. It provided office space for the administration of the program. From the conception of the program the church ensured that its central purpose of sharing Christ with these youth was not stifled. Sharing the gospel had to be done from a life style perspective, but it was still done. Since these youth were high risked it was necessary to provide a support counseling network for them. The church again through its counseling and Steven Ministries were able to provide those links. As youth were empowered though this program they were introduced to the youth ministries that took place on Friday nights.

The integration of these transforming high risked youth, with the existing churched youth was a struggle for the Chesta Peak Community church. In spite of the struggle, they developed a workable solution. These high risked youth started as a separate group. Then they were gradually introduced to the other youth. This had to be worked out carefully but in time the integration was effected. Today the "Fresh Start" ministry has grown into a fully supported agency of the church. The ministry is funded partially by the Canadian government and partially by the contracts that the program secures. It is a model of how a church can develop ministries with the proper strategic links to move people from unbeliever to believer. The program has also expanded from just working with one service provider to several. These service providers form other important aspects of the agency network that are directly related to the Chesta Peak Community Church.

Rails refer to the strategic links between a pre-evangelistic ministry like a day care, a gospel music festival or whatever, that lead people to the next logical step in their path to meeting Christ. In the last chapter we spoke of the need to link pre-evangelistic activities with other ministries so that there is a clear progression that move people from the community into the Church. To borrow Carl George's concept of "fishing pool," pre-evangelistic activities can be seen as fishing pools. Fishing pools are large group activities that are designed to help people connect to the church and build relationships. Once this is done rails are other groups or ministries that logically flow out of these fishing pools. An example of a fishing pool activity would be an Alpha celebration supper. A rail from this supper would be an invitation for the people attending the supper to sign up and attend the ten weeks Alpha course.

The most important idea in this section on rails is for churches to understand that every assimilation activity in which they are engaged should be purposeful. In other words each activity must lead some where.

The great philosopher Plato speaks of the danger of allowing passion to go unbridled. He said passion is like a wild horse it needs to be bridled by knowledge. One of the mistakes that churches often make is to fail to follow the wisdom of that statement. When people become passionate about ministry it is essential to direct that passion with knowledge. If this does not happen well meaning ministries can develop everywhere without the infra-structure or thought out strategy to sustain them and make them effective. Many churches fall victim to that problem. The example of the day care center given above is one such example. If at the onset of that ministry enough strategic thought was given to how this ministry would relate to the church and how the audience being reached by this ministry would be integrated into the church, proper rails could have been developed. It is much more difficult to correct the course of a fully developed ministry to include proper rails . Often times when churches try to refocus such ministries a falling out tends to happen. This happens because some people will inevitably feel betrayed because they think the ministry is changing course mid stream.

A much better way to go is to develop ministry teams comprised of people with visionary and strategic planning gifts. The visionaries are often the people of great passion. They are ready to start a ministry in spite of the fact that the proper ground work is not yet done. Strategic thinkers on the other hand will want to think things through properly. They will want to answer the question how will this ministry be linked to the overall church. Strategic thinkers will want to know how will people move from this ministry to becoming fully integrated into the life of the church. Ministries should not be developed as separate entities. They should keep in mind the whole picture. Every ministry must be seen as a vital part of the whole. If this is the case then ministries must have interdependent links to other ministries. These links are rails. They must be thought out before hand, otherwise imposing them latter on becomes quite difficult.

In the case of the Welsh family they could see quite clearly what their next step was after attending the stress management seminar. They needed to enrol in the 12 weeks small group on stress management. Just think, if this stress management seminar was offered without proper thought given to strategic links. It would have been executed. The participants would have left. They would have probably benefitted from the weekend information. But who knows what would have happened to them later on? There is no telling that they would be either connected to Christ or his church after that weekend. But because proper thought went into planning the event, the link was clear. The Welsh family knew what step to take next.

Key Concepts

Rails: Rails refer to the strategic links between a pre-evangelistic ministry like a day care, a gospel music festival or what ever, that lead people to the next logical step in their path to meeting Christ.

Fishing Pools: Fishing pools are large group activities that are designed to help people connect to the church and build relationships.

The Alpha Course: The Alpha Course was developed by Nikki Gumbel. It is a ten weeks introduction to Christianity course. It is built on a hospitality model of ministry. A supper is provided before each week's lesson. The course starts and ends with what is called a celebration supper. This is a time when new people are invited to a night of laughter, food and a brief introduction to the Alpha course. The Alpha course is available through Cook's Communication Ministry.

For Reflection and Action

1. What "fishing pool" activities does your church have to attract new people?
2. If your church has some fishing pool activities, how does it move people from that point to the next logical step in their faith search?
3. If your church does not have fishing pool activities, based on your assessment of your church and community what are some fishing pool events that your church could offer?

Owen Facey

Roll out the red carpet

CHAPTER 4

ASSIMILATION AND FIRST IMPRESSION MINISTRIES

Over the next several weeks Pat, Nancy, Tim and Dianne became very good friends. They had regular supper barbecues. Sometimes they even went to the movies together. One Saturday evening, at one of the couples, what was becoming regular weekend ritual - a Saturday evening barbecue, Tim asked Pat and Nancy what they thought about coming with them to church the next day. After all they were already attending church, just not on Sundays. They were attending Dr. Keene's stress management course. Pat looked at Tim and chided, "you must be kidding - me church." That was the end of talk about church. Tim thought he should not push the issue.

After supper that evening, both couples retired to their own homes. Pat and Nancy decided to spend the rest of the evening quietly. They sat watching television together. "Pat," Nancy said, "the last few months have really been some of the best times we have had. Look, this move almost broke us apart, but now look what has happened. That stress management course was just what we needed. After leaving all our friends in Fort Lauderdale I did not know what to think. But Tim and Dianne have really been good friends." Pat was fairly silent. He was thinking over what Nancy was saying. "What do you believe is happening to us," Pat asked? "I really do not know. One thing I know we seem to be getting along much better. At least we are not as stressed. And look we even have a quiet evening that we can just sit down together," Nancy said. "Yes, things are much better. You know Nancy I have been thinking about Tim's invitation." "What do you mean," Nancy said. "I don't know but maybe we should check out their church." "Maybe," Nancy said.

The next day Pat and Nancy decided to surprise their neighbor. They showed up at church. As soon as they entered the church's parking lot, they were met with something different. There were so many cars. They did not believe how many people actually came to the church. It was only after, that they found out that the church had an attendance of eight hundred people. There were parking attendants right there to show them where to park. As they walked to the door of the church, there were greeters, welcoming them. "Do you mind if I quickly show you where some of the vital areas are in the church?," one of the greeters asked. "Certainly", Nancy said. They were shown where the rest rooms, nursery and Sunday school classes were. Nancy thought "this is nice, nothing like needing to use the bathroom and not knowing where to find it."

As they came to the worship center, there were ushers there guiding them to a place to sit. "You seem to be new" one of the ushers said. "What brought you here today?" Pat answered, "we have some friends who attend here, Tim and Dianne Lewis." "Oh, Tim. Look, they are sitting right over there, would you want to sit by them?" "Yes," Pat said. What a surprise for Tim and Dianne.

First Impression Ministries

You probably have heard it said, "first impressions are lasting." This is true even in your church. When new people attend church for the first time it is critical that they have a good experience. If they do not, they will not return, or the chance of them returning is very slim. Richard Bast observes that two out of three people who visit a church twice within a brief period of time are more likely to join the congregation

(1988:14). Church of God writer, Oral Withrow shares a similar sentiment. He said, "of the persons who visit, three out of ten should be involved in the church within twelve months of their first visit (1991:94). Both these authors have some common concerns. Newcomers must be assimilated early in the process if they will become active in the local church. A critical part of the assimilation process is "first impression ministries." These are ministries designed to reach out to visitors when they attend church for the first time.

Some of the more obvious first impression ministries are usher and greeter ministries, and parking lot attendants. It is helpful that these people be trained to understand the needs of visitors when they attend church for the first time. It is also important that they see their ministries as evangelistic. The form of evangelism that ushers, greeters and parking lot attendants are engaged in is pre-evangelism. They are helping to break down the defenses and negative hang-ups that visitors might have about church. Care must be taken to help the visitors feel comfortable and develop a desire to return.

The more non obvious "first impression ministries" revolve around what happens during the worship service and after the service. A helpful step in helping visitors to develop a desire to return is welcoming them in an un-embarrassing way during the service. It is not necessary to make visitors stand up and introduce themselves, or wear outrageous visitor pins. The pastor or some body designated can easily welcome visitors, thank them for coming, and invite them back to worship another time without making them conspicuous. This welcome should be done from the pulpit.

One of the absolutely necessary thing to do during the service, or during the time of the visitor being at church, is to get certain personal information from them, like their names, sex, possible age range, address and attendance status. This information can be secured in several ways. Visitors could be asked to sign a guest book by the greeters when they first enter through the doors. A memo pad could be passed out during the service, that all the attenders are encouraged to sign and pass down the rows. Some churches refer to this pad as a "Know Your Neighbor Pad." Whatever it is called, each church must develop a system by which they secure personal information. This is the only way that effective follow-up can be done.

This pad should provide the following information: names, address, phone number, sex, possible age range and attendance status - that is visitor or regular attender. This pad is usually picked up and the information entered into a database. More will be said about the data base in a future section. It is critical to allow visitors to know what you will be doing with this information. Therefore when the welcome is given, care should be taken to tell the people that the information they provide is to help the church better minister to their needs though follow-up. Visitors can then choose whether or not to fill this out. It is my experience that most usually fill it out.

Other "first impression" things that can be done in the service, concern the design of each service with the visitor in mind. Use overhead projection system so that songs are easily followed and sung. Cut down on the use of too much "churchy" language. It is helpful for the congregation to be trained to look out for people who are visiting, so that when the service is over, a visitor is not left standing in a corner by him/herself. Members should make an effort to speak to visitors. Maybe even invite them out for lunch.

On Monday another series of first impression ministries begin. A letter should be sent to visitors, by the senior pastor, thanking them for attending, and offering the services of the church to them. An invitation should be given to them to return. A helpful ministry to develop is a first time callers ministry. This is a group of people who are specially trained to call visitors within a forty eight hour period after they have attended worship. This call is important. In it the caller answers any questions that visitors might have, finds out what brought them, uncover any area of dissatisfaction with the service, along with areas that the visitor liked. This information is necessary for the continued evaluation of the services.

The goal of these first impression ministries is to help people develop strong links with the church. Business consultant, Tom Peters says "in order for customer experience to lead to repeat business, an emotional link must develop between the customer and the product or service. There is a large affective component to service" (1994:240). While this is a market driven idea, the church can learn a valuable lesson from what Peters is saying. If secular companies have figured out that for people to keep buying a certain product they need to fall in love with it, how much more does the church have a message of love to communicate. Love is the message Christians preach. Christ's coming and dying were all about love. Unfortunately when visitors attend our churches they are treated less than lovely. "First impression" ministries are designed to help visitors feel loved.

Key Concepts

First Impression Ministries: These are ministries designed to reach out to visitors when they attend church for the first time with the goal of helping them to feel loved and valued.

Emotional Link: An emotional link describes the process of helping people have a good feeling about the church the first time they attend. In other words fall in love with it.

First time Caller Ministry: It is a ministry designed to make calls within a forty eight hour period to people who visit the church for the first time. These callers seek to thank people for coming and gather feed back about the service.

Welcome Letter: A welcome letter can be a form letter done by the senior pastor, that is sent to visitors thanking them for attending church. More than one letter should be done and rotated periodically. Otherwise they become stale. Also it is more meaningful if the pastor or persons assigned to send out these letters put a personal note on the letters each week. This adds a more personal touch.

Know Your Neighbor Pad: This is a feedback tool that is passed out in each service for people to fill out. The information needed on this is name, address, sex, age category, category of attender e.g. visitor or regular. It is also important to indicate on this card whether people need a pastoral call. Some churches have what is called a "Friendship and Communications Card." It does the same thing.

For Reflection and Action

1. What "first impression" ministries does your church have?
2. If it does not have any how will you get started?
3. How does your church gather personal information from new people?
4. How is newcomer follow-up done in your church?

A Guide to Assimilation in the Local Church

Who are we?

CHAPTER 5

ASSIMILATION AND CHURCH IDENTITY

The worship service was very different. After all the last time Pat and Nancy attended church was when they were teenagers. That was about fifteen years ago. This service was very different from what they remembered. The people seemed to be enjoying the music. The music was projected on an overhead screen by a video projector. The songs were lively. The atmosphere in the building was similar to a concert. The light was dim and at certain parts of the program the color of the lighting changed. That was evident when the drama team came on.

As Pat and Nancy went home that day, the only thought that dominated their minds was how different this service was. They were left with a warm positive feeling. The sermon that morning was also very relevant to where they were in their lives. Pastor Ben spoke about ways to enrich your marriage. Whether or not Pat and Nancy would return was something to be decided. During the following week the topic of church would come up periodically.

One evening Pat and Nancy sat down to unwind after a long and busy day of work. The subject of church again came up. "Why do you think that service last Sunday was so different," Nancy asked Pat. "I have been thinking about that," Pat said, "but you know I am not quite sure. Maybe it had something to do with the music, maybe with the drama. It could even be with the atmosphere. I don't know. I think Ben's sermon was also very relevant. Or, what should I say, maybe because we know Tim and Dianne. That made us feel comfortable. I think we should go back a few more times, and see if this was a show, or a special Sunday." Nancy agreed to that.

The next several Sundays they went back and they left with similar impressions. In fact another element about the church struck them. On one of those Sundays, one of the members invited them out for lunch after the service. Before they knew it, they had attended church about four weeks in a row. The fourth week as the "Know-Your-Neighbor Pad" was being passed around, Nancy held on to it for a while. "Pat do you think we are still visitors?" "What do you mean," Pat asked? "Afer all we have been attending for a while now. We could sign that we are regular attenders" Nancy said. "What ever . . ." Pat said. That Sunday for the first time Pat and Nancy signed that they were regular attenders at the church.

The next week they received a call from the church inviting them to a hospitality party for newcomers to the church. Pat and Nancy did not think much of it so they agreed to attend. At this hospitality party an opportunity was given for guests to meet eight other newcomers to the church. The evening was very laid back. They had finger food, watched a video about "who the church is," and played games. They were also given an opportunity to ask any questions that they had. The couple that hosted the party, in their home, was obviously very knowledgeable about the church. They answered the questions rather easily. At the end of the party an interest finder was circulated. On it was written all the different growth opportunities that existed in the church. There was a newcomers series for those who were new to the church but were already Christians. There was also another group for those who were just searching but were not Christians. The group was encouraged to choose one. Pat and Nancy chose the one that was for those who were searching.

Owen Facey

Moving from a Casual Attender to a Part of the Body of Christ

It is critical for every church to have a clear plan to help people move from just merely attending church to becoming a vital part of the body of Christ. This is the part of assimilation that can quickly break down for many churches. It is easy to focus so much on getting people in and when they finally come in they just sit, because there is not a clearly communicated path to help them make the commitments that are necessary to become a fully functioning part of the body of Christ.

Once newcomers indicate that they are regular attenders, the church must have some mechanism to formally recognize their commitment. One way to do this is to have something like a hospitality party or a newcomers' potluck. In these settings the atmosphere should be laid back. It should be geared to helping newcomers know more about the church, make some other personal connections with others in the church, and see what the church has available for their growth. It is also necessary at the parties or potlucks to encourage newcomers to make a further commitment. This commitment should be the next logical step for them in their spiritual journey. For those who are not Christians the option should be given for them to be in a group that helps them explore their faith. A good group for this is the Alpha course. Those who are already Christians, the opportunity should be given to them to enter into some kind of discipleship oriented group. The ones who might not be ready for any of the above two, some other need based small groups might be options. The critical thing is not to allow newcomers to stagnate in their spiritual process.

One of the paths that some churches have employed in the assimilation process is to design a series of classes that help people move from the outside of the church to the inside and back outside for ministry. These classes are variously called, "Christianity 101, Christianity 102, etc. Rick Warren of Saddle Back Community Church is instrumental in helping churches understand that each church must have a clear strategy to move people from being non-Christians to people of mission. It is on his ideas that the philosophy of this section is based.

Other churches refer to these classes as "Major League Christianity." The first class is entitled "Getting into the Game." This class is designed to be introductory. It covers such areas as the mission, vision, core values of the church, a gospel presentation, expectations, and outlines a path to Christian maturity. The second class is designed to move people from first base to second base. This is moving people from membership to maturity. It covers all the essential elements that will help newcomers become fully functioning members in God's church. The third class seeks to move people from maturity to ministry. Here people discover their spiritual gifts, personality profiles, and role preferences. In essence they discover their ministry profiles. The final class in this series seeks to move people from ministry to mission. This is helping people to discover and function according to what they are called to be and do.

For newcomers the advantages are many once they have been engaged in the process described above. First, if newcomers are not Christians they will become Christians, in an informed way. This means they will have all the information necessary for them to make the right decisions about becoming Christians. This is critical since it moves counter to the idea that people should just make hasty decisions to become Christians, without the support systems in place to see them discipled. Evangelism in the past has majored on quick decisions. Consequently many of the people who made decisions to become Christians ended up not lasting. The relationship element was not there. The church did not provide the discipleship support systems. For the same reason others who became Christians, stagnated.

Second, new persons get a good understanding about the church and what is expected of them. This is identity forming. Newcomers have an opportunity to key into the vision and mission of the church. Once they have bought in, they will now help the church to fulfill its vision and mission. When people buy into a vision or a cause, it is difficult for them to leave. This is assimilation at its highest. It you want to close the back door to your church get people enrolled in the vision and mission of the church.

Developing a Clear Vision for Your Church

The issue of vision is a very confusing subject for many churches. It is confusing for many reasons. First, there is the question of clearly defining what vision really is. Second, is the issue of determining how a vision is formed. Is vision a figment of the imagination, or is it something solidly grounded somewhere? Is a vision just personal or can it be shared? These are just some of the questions that cause great confusion for some churches. It is necessary for each church that is interested in establishing a clear identity to answer the above questions. If the leadership of these churches is confused about vision, then it is fair to conclude that the people will also be confused about the same.

The last decade has witnessed the writing of many books on vision. Many organizations have crafted vision statements. One of the dangers of vision statements is that they can quickly become an intellectual exercise. Robert Quinn in his book *Deep Change* notes that "though vision statements are now common in most large organizations, vision is not"

(1996:195). The primary reason being, vision can easily become a mental exercise.

The intent of this section is not to become submerged in the various pieces of literature concerning vision. But for the purpose of this project, George Barna's and Burt Nanus' understanding of vision have been adopted. According to Barna "vision . . . is a clear mental image of a preferable future imparted by God to his chosen servants and is based upon an accurate understanding of God, self and circumstances" (1992:28). Another way of defining vision is what Nanus sees as "a realistic, credible, attractive future of your organization" (1992:8).

The above definitions have several implications. First, there is an implied dissatisfaction with the present. This dissatisfaction gives rise to a picture of a preferable tomorrow. Barna notes "vision is never about maintaining the status quo. Vision is about stretching reality to extend beyond the existing state"

(1992:29). Second, a vision for God's Church must come from God. This suggests that a vision for the church must be born in prayer, and out of a close relationship with God. Barna observes that the future of God's kingdom work is far too important for leaders to rely on their own innate abilities to accomplish God's work (1992:30).

A third aspect of a good vision is that it must be in touch with reality. A vision for God's Church arises out of a good understanding of God and what he wants to do in his Church. A vision also arises out of a good understanding of ones ministry context. It would be futile to have a vision to feed the homeless in ones community, if there are not homeless people in the community. Finally, a good vision must reflect the strengths and passions of the leader, and the ministering community who will seek to fulfill this vision.

James Sanders, in his book *Canon and Community, A Guide to Canonical Criticism,* discusses the role of the clergy or leader in hearing God's voice anew for new times. He suggests that the process of hearing God's voice anew must be done through, what he calls, "an interpretive triangle" (1988:69-77). One angle of the triangle represents God's voice to the leader, another angle represents the text or scriptures, and the third angle represents the context in which one lives. While Sanders was speaking of a hermeneutical process, this model has much to add to how a vision is formed. Vision is being understood here as a form of interpreting and reinterpreting reality, such that the scriptures are spoken with freshness to different contexts. In this sense vision is a hermeneutical process.

I have taken the liberty to digress on this triangle to develop a vision triangle. The first angle of this triangle represents what God is saying through scripture. A vision for God's people must be first grounded in the scriptures. The second angle represents the context in which the vision is to be carried out. Careful research must be done to understand ones community in order to minister effectively in that context. This will enable the vision to be relevant. The third angle has to do with the leader and the community who are carrying out this vision. A careful vision audit must be done, isolating the strengths and weaknesses of this community. The leader must be aware of his or her strengths and weaknesses as well. The combination of the community's and leader's strengths and weaknesses, and the voice of God through scripture, should lead to the realization of a vision.

Once the vision of the church has been crafted, the church should now begin to focus on how it will accomplish this vision? This question will lead to a discovery of the churches purpose or mission. The mission of the church describes what the church is called to do. The bible is clear on what the church is called to do if one examines such passages as Matt.28:19-20 - the great commission, Luke 4:18 - Jesus conceived mission and other such passages. Churches might develop a variation of the mandate described in scripture, but essentially the purpose of God's church must be reaching the lost and building up the kingdom of God.

A further step might be necessary. This step is called strategy. Strategy describes the vehicle through which a church will accomplish its mission and vision. This is the clear path that leads a person from being a non-Christian to a fully discipled, and contributing member of the body of Christ. It is the same process that was outlined above as Major league Christianity and Christianity 101.

Once a strategy is conceived it must be communicated clearly and often. Not only should this communication take place with the newcomers, it should also happen with the existing members in the congregation. Newcomers need to know where they are going in terms of their own maturity. Existing members in the church can sometimes become complacent the longer they are in the church. The way to keep both fully immersed in the overall identity of the church is to have every ministry reflecting the vision, mission and strategy of the church. This will mean that a church will of necessity go through some kind of ministry realignment process once it has determined its mission, vision and strategy. The alignment process seeks to ensure that all ministries are connected to the purpose of the church and are a part of its overall strategy. Some helpful resources in developing church identity, are *Moving from Vision to Action*, by George Barna, *Total Quality Ministry* by Walt Kalestad and Steve Shey.

Key Concepts

Identity: Identity describes the key elements that distinguish one particular church from another. Elements such as vision, mission, core values and strategies are essential for identity formation.

Hospitality Parties: These are informal parties held for newcomers. They are hosted by different members of a particular church. They are designed to welcome newcomers into the life of the church and help them take the next step in their spiritual pilgrimage.

Newcomers' Potluck: These are fellowship opportunities hosted by a local church to welcome new people into the life of the church. They tend to be bigger than a hospitality party, but the purposes are the same.

Major League Christianity: This is a discipleship series designed by the East Side Church of God, Swift

Current, Saskatchewan that aims to move people from being non-Christians to mature, fully functioning parts of the local church and the kingdom of Christ.

For Reflection and Action

1. What makes your church different from other churches in your community? (e.g. vision, mission, core values).
2. How are new members enrolled in the identity of your church?
3. How are people brought to maturity in your church?

Owen Facey

Making a difference - this is what I was born to do.

CHAPTER 6

FULLY ASSIMILATED- FINDING MY PLACE IN MINISTRY

Pat and Nancy attended the Major League Christianity - Getting into the Game Seminar. The seminar was offered on a Saturday. It went from 9 a.m. to 4 p.m. The first hour was a continental breakfast. There were about thirty people at this seminar. "This church must really have something going," Nancy said. "I can't believe that all these people are new. I did not know that so many new people actually show up at church. I wonder how often do they have these classes?" Pat decided that he would ask. "Mr. Cocrane, can I ask you a question," Pat said. Mr Cocrane was the seminar leader. "Sure he said, what can I do for you." "How often do you run this seminar?" "We try to do them every quarter." Pat and Nancy were even more impressed. They could not believe that in three months thirty new people actually showed up at the church and were making a similar decision as they were making.

In the first session Mr Cocrane outlined the goals of the course. The course is designed to be offered in a one day seminar. It is consisted of six sessions. Each session is about one hour long. The course has four goals. First, to begin the process of effectively integrating new people into the life of the church. Second, to introduce new people to the strategy for spiritual growth at the church. Third, to help clarify people's commitment to Christ and the church. Fourth, to help class members take the next logical step in order to enhance their spiritual growth. "Do you understand all those things that Mr, Cocrane just said Pat?," Nancy asked. "I am not sure but I suppose we are here already, so let's see what it is all about."

A Guide to Assimilation in the Local Church

An outline of the sessions was also given. Session one is basically orientation and focus. Session two deals with knowing your identity. In this session a brief history of the organization that the church is apart of is given. Session three deals with the local history of the church - how it started and from where it has come. Session four is about the vision, mission, core values and strategy of the church. Session five deals with growing up in Christ. In this session what it means to become a Christian is given. The final session is about stewardship and expectations.

"I think the seminar was very insightful," Nancy said. At least we certainly know what the church is about." "It was also interesting to know what churches in general are suppose to be about" Pat noted. The couple drove home quietly after the seminar. That evening as they sat down for their nightly ritual of watching T.V. and "vegging," they talked over some of the things they learned at the seminar. Pat was particularly interested in the explanation Mr. Cocrane gave about what it means to be a Christian. The question that rested on his mind was how should he respond? "Nancy you know, I have been thinking about changing my life," Pat said. "What do you mean," Nancy asked? "You know, doing what Cocrane said. Ask God to forgive me from my sins and sign up for the other seminars," Tim said. "I don't believe it. I have been thinking the same thing" Nancy said. That night both of them, in the quiet of their home, committed their lives to Christ. It was the beginning of a new life for them. They also signed up to attend the other seminars. The second one was on discipleship, and discovering your place in ministry.

My Ministry Profile

I am sure you must have heard the term "being like a square peg in a round hole." The point of this little saying is that people can often find themselves working or serving in positions for which they are not suited. The important process that each church must undertake is to develop a plan that helps people discover their gifts, passion and place of service. When people are ministering according to their ministry profiles they are more fulfilled and it takes less time to motivate them.

If one goes back to the definition of assimilation, one will remember that the concept has to do with integrating people into the body of Christ and releasing them to serve. Helping members to discover their ministry profiles is precisely about integrating people into the body of Christ and equipping them to serve passionately.

There are many resource materials available that help people discover their ministry profiles. Here are a few: *Houts' Inventory of Spiritual Gifts*, *Wagner-Modified Houts Inventory of Spiritual Gifts*, *The*

Wesley Spiritual Gifts Questionnaire and the Network Kit. These are just a few. There is also a combination profile, produced by Mel Carbonell that seeks to relate spiritual gifts with personality types. It is entitled *Uniquely You*. This resource has four parts, personality profile, multi-purpose personality profile, relationships profile and spiritual gifts profile. Another personality testing resource that can be employed is the Personality Tree by Florence Littauer. A resource that is valuable in helping people discover their passion for ministry is *What you do best in the Body of Christ*, by Bruce Bugbee. It might be necessary to adapt the questions he outlined to your own church and ministry context.

Enough cannot be said about the importance of showing people a clear path to spiritual maturity. Often times churches tend to treat the Christian experience as involving one solid decision. This is the decision one makes to follow Christ. Once that decision is made then all ones spiritual needs have been taken care of. A statement like the above is indeed extreme and undoubtedly no church would admit to making such a statement. Yet the truth is many churches tend to act on that assumption.

Canadian sociologist Reginald Bibby, notes that churches that want to effectively reach the lost must change the assumptions they make about ministry. One such assumption is to view leading people to Christ as more than a single decision. According to Bibby "results take time" (1992:256). This assumption refers to the fact that coming to faith must be conceived as a process. This is a caution against the kind of evangelism that was done in previous years where people were encouraged to "make a decision," as illustrated in the ideas behind Billy Graham's *Decision Magazine* and his radio program "The Hour of Decision" (Salter 1996:104).

One decision might not be an adequate response to the complexity of their faith search. The truth about ones faith walk is that it involves many decisions. One might need to make a decision to first become involved in something the church offers. Another decision is needed to attend church for the first time. A decision also needs to be made in committing ones life to Christ. It is also possible that one will fall, and so another decision of re-commitment might be necessary. Young Christains want the assurance that the Church will be there with them in their struggles.

It is not enough to get people saved and then leave them. Focus must be given to the entire process. This process includes the following stages. First there is the connection phase. This is where bridge building ministries are done in the community that seek to build relationships and raise spiritual questions. The second stage has to do with first impression ministries that help new people feel connected to the church the moment they attend. The third phase is helping them to come to a place of commitment to Christ and his Church. Once that has been done the person needs to be involved in a discipleship process. In this discipleship process, members must understand what it means to be a Christ follower. They must discover their ministry profiles. Finally, they must be mentored into a suitable place of service. To miss any one of these phases is to short circuit the person's spiritual growth. This can lead to stagnation and ineffectiveness

Key Concepts

The Church as an Organization: This is the denomination or movement of which a local church is a part. It is important for newcomers to know the history of the particular denomination. It solidifies identity.

The Church Local: This is the individual churches that carry out ministries in the community.

Ministry Profile: It is the combination of one's spiritual gifts, passion for ministry, personality type and ministry preference. This profile helps people to minister according to their calling.

For Reflection and Action

1. Does your church have a method or strategy that help people discover their ministry profile?
2. How are people enrolled for ministry in your Church? Is it based on ministry profile or mere availability?
3. If it is by mere availability what steps do you need to take to move to the place where people minister according to their ministry profiles?
4. What effect on your church do you think you would see if people begin to minister according to their gifts, i.e. in recruitment, motivation, fulfillment and effectiveness?

A Guide to Assimilation in the Local Church

"Closing the Back Door"

CHAPTER 7

ASSIMILATION AND YOUR BACKDOOR

It has now been a year and a half since Pat and Nancy started attending church. A lot has happened since that time. The friendship they have developed with Tim and Dianne has continued to grow. Added to all of that they have developed new friends at the church. Who could have guessed a year and a half ago, that the struggling couple who was on the verge of divorce would have had their lives straightened out in this manner. Pat and Nancy have often reflected that church was the last place that they would have shown up. But now church is the thing that has made the real difference in their lives. Maybe we should say Jesus, through his church, has made the difference in their lives. But it was not long before the couple faced a major mountain. It was a mountain that they found very difficult to climb.

Church seemed to be going great for Pat and Nancy. On the outside their relationship also appeared to be going well. But something was happening to them. It was hard to explain. The enthusiasm that they had about church was waning a bit. They found themselves arguing again, much like they used to before they started going to church. Over the last year and a half, after attending all those initial classes offered by the church, both Pat and Nancy have been engaged in an apprenticeship relationship. They were being developed to be small group leaders. But now, they did not care too much even to attend their small group meeting. This slide started with Pat and it soon affected Nancy.

It was Saturday morning. The usual routine for Pat is to sleep in a little and then head out for his small group meeting that started at ten. This particular

Saturday morning Pat did not care to go so he continued sleeping in. Two Saturday mornings past and he did the same thing. Both Pat and Nancy still attended church on Sundays however, but something was happening.

It was now the third week since Pat had not shown up at his group meeting. That Saturday afternoon Pat's group leader, Harry called. Harry wanted to have lunch with Pat. The date was set for the following Tuesday. At lunch Harry expressed the group's concern for Pat. They were praying for both Pat and Nancy regularly because they noticed that something was wrong. Pat could hardly believe that his group cared so much about them. For the first time Pat broke down and shared what has been eating away at his heart and also the relationship with his wife.

Both Pat and Nancy had been married for five years. For the last three years they have been trying to have children, but were not successful. When they both became Christians they thought God would answer their prayers and give them a child. They really believed God for this. About four months ago, Nancy went to the doctor and came back with exciting news, she was pregnant. Pat and Nancy were ecstatic. They choose not to tell anyone, because they felt it was a little too early. As hard as the news was to keep they held on to it. Just one month ago Nancy miscarried. Words cannot express how painful this has been for them. This experience has brought them face to face with some of the toughest questions that people wrestle with about God.

"You know Harry the question I have is this. Where is God when all these screw-ups in life are happening? Does he really answer prayer, or do people just become lucky or unlucky in life? If God is good and loving, why do things like these happen? O, did I say the question I have? I suppose I have many questions." Harry offered what he could to help Pat, but he left that meeting knowing that their group was going to have to pray harder for Pat and Nancy.

One month had now past and Pat and Nancy were still struggling with this miscarriage and all those theological questions. Last week was the first time they missed church. Both of them were not attending their small group meetings anymore and now for the first time they had also missed church. The following week they also missed church, and the following week. After the third Sunday of missing church, They received a letter from Pastor Ben. The letter basically stated that he noticed that they had missed church for the last three Sundays, and he was praying for them. Furthermore he offered his help if they ever needed it. "Do you mean Pastor Ben would notice that we are missing from church, in spite of the fact that over eight hundred people attend the church," Nancy said. That was a little overwhelming, but the reality was they had missed church and they were missed.

Pat and Nancy continued to drift. It was now the fifth week that they had missed church. Harry had called a few times. Tim and Dianne had also been over a few times but nothing seemed to be working. After the fifth week of missing church, Nancy got a phone call from the Church. The person identified himself as a member of the church pastoral care group. For the next half an hour Nancy poured out her heart on the phone. That phone call was just what she needed. For so long she had kept all this pain inside, now she felt like she had released it.

An appointment was set up between Pat, Nancy and members from the pastoral care team. The appointment was for that Thursday evening. On Thursday Joe and his wife Ceile came over to visit. Both Joe and Cecile were lay leaders from the church. The couples shared freely, however very superficially. Then Joe broke in "you know Pat and Nancy our hearts ache for what you are going through. Fifteen years ago we were at the same place. We wanted to have children so badly. We were both Christians. We believed that God would answer our prayers. He did. Only for us to have lost our son to Sudden Infant Death Syndrome (SIDS). Worst yet we still have not been able to have any more Children." "So how do you deal with that," Pat asked? The rest of the evening was spend exchanging ideas. Pat and Nancy were back at church the following Sunday. Something must have worked.

Back Door Ministries

The need for back door ministries arises out of some of my observations in ministry. As new people are added to our church, primarily those who are transferring in from other churches, it is one of my responsibilities to talk with them. I am usually left somewhat troubled after talking with them, because I often hear this refrain. "I have left that church for so long and no one has ever called me or come to visit me. It seems no one ever knew or cared that I was ever there and no one really missed me when I showed up no longer." A statement like this can have many implications. First, when people become dissatisfied and leave a church it seems they are always looking for someone to blame. So the general church gets blamed. Second, the degree to which people become assimilated into a fellowship depends on how willing they are to be assimilated. Sometimes a church tries everything it knows to assimilate some people and they still are not assimilated. Third, churches do not care enough to go the second mile with people who are struggling. Consequently when these people leave they are not followed-up on. This last reason provides the general assumption for back door ministries

Some of the biblical examples that could be cited for back door ministries are the following. In Acts fifteen verses thirty six through forty one, an account is given concerning Paul's second missionary journey. Barnabas wanted to take John Mark on this journey but Paul did not. The scripture notes "Paul kept insisting that they should not take him along who had deserted them in Pamphylia and had not gone with them to the work" (vs.38). Later on, one notes a "sharp" disagreement arose between them. The result, Paul took Silas and Barnabas took Mark.

It is obvious that Barnabas saw something more in Mark that Paul did not necessarily see. Whatever it was that Barnabas saw in Mark, one thing is obvious, Barnabas wanted to give Mark a second chance. Back door ministries, in many ways, is about giving people a second chance.

Another biblical example that could be cited is John chapter twenty one. There is much disagreement among scholars whether this passage is really authentic since it was not found in some of the original manuscripts (Beasley-Murray 1987:395). The point I wish to make here however, has to do with the messages this passage communicates about back door ministries. Several messages could be highlighted.

First, Jesus was sensitive to the disciples' pain. The situation can be summarized in the following way. Jesus was now crucified. The disciples had drifted. They were disappointed that Jesus had let them down. Simon Peter, Thomas and Nathanael were gone fishing. Then Jesus arrived on the scene. Jesus went to where they were. This act offered the disciples the gift of his presence (vs.1).

Second, He helped them to believe in themselves again by helping them to catch a large amount of fish (vs. 6 & 7). This is significant because the disciples were toiling all night and did not catch anything. They were frustrated and beaten but Jesus encouraged them.

Third, Jesus had fellowship with them (vs.12). Many times when people are struggling they pull away from the fellowship because of shame. They are afraid of being judged or misunderstood. Fellowship often communicates the message of understanding that these people need. Jesus provided the gift of understanding for these disciples.

Fourth, Jesus re-empowered Peter. Jesus asked Peter a question. "Do you love me more than these?" Once Jesus got the desired answer from Peter, He re-empowered him to take care of "His flock" (vs.15-17).

I think Jesus could have given up on these disciples, but He did not. He went the extra mile to bring them back into fellowship with him. Back door ministries seek to provide opportunities to people who are struggling, to be reunited with the fellowship. It is also engaged in preventative care which help to keep people connected both to the fellowship and Christ. The ministries involved could be classified under two areas, compassionate and follow up ministries.

Compassionate Ministries

Compassionate ministries seek to uncover pockets of pain in the church and community and design a plan to address them. Logan and Short suggest that one of the first steps in starting compassionate ministries is to uncover the pain in your church (1994:61). It is important to start in your church since wounded people who have found healing, sometimes make the best candidates to form a ministry team to help others who have been similarly wounded. Also having wounded people who have found healing ministering in the capacity of compassionate ministries adds credibility to the process. Many times people who have suffered pain want to know that the person who is seeking to help them has also experienced similar pain. This gives the assurance to the ones needing help that, at least, they are understood.

In order to uncover the pain in one's church, a four step process could be followed. These steps are ones laid out by Logan and Short. They are listening, relating, debriefing, and investigating (1994:61). These are the same steps that could be followed in designing compassionate ministries for the wider community.

In listening a select group of people with the passion and gifted-ness for compassionate ministries set their hearts and minds to listen to God and the church. As they pray they ask some of the following questions. What are the issues of concern to the people in our church? What are some of the areas of their pain? What are they saying about their pain? What are some of the issues behind what they are saying? What might God be saying about how some of these issues can be addressed? Who are these people who have suffered such hurts? This final question will help to determine other potential people to be on the compassionate ministries team.

In order to compile some data on what is being heard, it would be necessary to develop some kind of feed back system. This system should help people express what they are feeling. Relate refers to building bridges with people in the church. This speaks of the pastor and team members, who are desiring to develop compassionate ministries, developing deeper relationships with congregation members. Sometimes it is in these relationships that certain deep needs are discovered. These friends can also become ears to the rest of the church. Church members tend to speak to other members about needs that they might have.

Debriefing speak of conducting exit poling. This area is primarily what follow-up ministries are about. Therefore it will be dealt with in the following section.

Investigating refers to discovering of hurts in the community. It also refers to the process of positioning the church to address such hurts. Much like the process in pre-evangelism, back door assimilation seeks to engage members in the process of gathering pertinent information from community agencies on the critical needs that people are facing in the community. Some of the agencies that could be a source for such information are schools, the Department of Social Services, Community Safe Shelters and the Police Department.

Follow-up Ministries

An important area of back door ministry is follow-up letters. Members could receive many kinds of letters. It they are absent from worship three Sundays in a row they should receive a missing in attendance letter. This letter aims at communicating to them that "their church family and pastors care about them." Sometimes members are away on holidays, or if you live in a farming community, it might be seeding or harvesting times so they are not in church; a specialized letter could be designed for them. The letter would say something to the effect that they are missed and the pastors are praying for them. The offer would also be made if they need any help to let the church know. If people are on holidays a letter could be sent expressing wishes of a happy and safe holiday.

When people miss five Sundays in a row a phone call should be made by a member from the absentee calling team. One of the goals here is to see if a visit would be necessary. If a visit is necessary, either a member from the absentee calling team, or depending on the concerns, a pastor should make the visit. If there is a problem why the person is not attending, the pastor or team member attempts to resolve it, and restore the person. If restoration is not possible then, an exit interview would be conducted. The attempt would be made to help the person find another church that might be more suitable to his or her needs. Note would also be taken as to why the person does not want to attend any longer.

A final type of letter would be needed if people miss nine weeks in a row. At this point a letter could be sent with an opportunity for absentees to declare their intentions. If they are switching churches it would be helpful to know. This letter would follow a visit that did not lead to restoration. In the letter, the door is left open for the person to return at any time. The nine weeks letter provides closure for people who want to transition from the church.

The steps in back door ministries are geared to provide members with as many opportunities as possible to find restoration. They are designed to bring those who are moving away from the rule of God, back under His rule. If restoration is not possible after all that effort, members cannot leave saying the church did not try to help. This is critical since a good community reputation is important for a local church.

Key Concepts

Back door Ministries: Back door ministries seek to provide opportunities to people who are struggling, to be reunited with the fellowship. It is also engaged in preventative ministries which help to keep people connected both to the fellowship and Christ.

Compassionate Ministries: These are ministries designed to help people restore balance in their lives. Such ministries, could be divorce Care, weight loss ministries, grief ministries just to name a few.

Follow-up Letters: These are a series of letters designed to help parishioners feel that the church really care's about them. It is important to note that some people do not like to receive such letters. If they make the request that these letters not be sent to them, that request should be honored. From experience, however, most people respond positively to such letters.

Exit Interview: These are interviews conducted with people who are leaving the church. The goal in these interviews is to hear the reason that lead to their wanting to leave. If restoration is possible the attempt should be made. If that is not possible, then these people should be given the opportunity to have some closure to their stay at the church. An open invitation should always be left for them to return at any time.

For Reflection and Action

1. What back door ministries does your church have?
2. How do you know when members are leaving your church?
3. What strategy do you have in place to help restore or make members who are leaving

transition more smoothly to another place of worship?

4. If you do not have back door ministries how could you get started?

Owen Facey

"Now I know!"

CHAPTER 8

STARTING THE PROCESS OF ASSIMILATION IN YOUR CHURCH

The first step in starting the assimilation process in your church is to take a good look at your church - church assessment. Richard Bast, in his book *Attracting New Members*, encourages congregations to do assessments which aim at discovering their strengths and weaknesses (1988:36). He recommends that congregations gather information concerning attendance, conversion, dropout rate, and means of member addition patterns for at least the last five years. Covering a five year span of time helps a congregation to see patterns of growth, decline or plateau.

Once this information is gathered a church should be able to tell its primary areas of weaknesses and strengths. These are the areas that will need to be addressed if a church is going to grow. The next step is to begin to ask the question why? Why are we declining or why are we stagnating? For some churches the question might be why are we growing? The church that is growing might need to seek to improve the strategies that are responsible for growth. The church that is declining will need to clearly articulate why it is declining. It will also need to determine what it needs to do to turn things around. The church that has plateaued will need to break out of certain comfort zones and begin to stretch so that it can move up from the plateau. At any rate careful church assessment must be done.

Another reason for church assessment is to help a church discover where it needs to invest its resources for the maximum return. One church will not be able to be all things to all people. In other words one church will not be able to cover the broad spectrum of ministries that the kingdom of God demands. Every church, based on people and financial resources will need to determine what it is good at, and seek to maximize that strength. Assessment helps a church to refine its focus and major on its strength.

Some resources that are available to help churches do internal assessment are the Natural Church Development questionnaire and the Precept instruments. Natural Church Development is a comprehensive tool developed by German theologian Christian Schwartz, after studying over one thousand churches across the world to find out what makes a healthy church. His conclusion was that there are eight essential characteristics: Empowering Leadership, Gift-oriented Ministry, Holistic Small Groups, Functional Structures, Need Based Evangelism, Dynamic Worship, Passionate Spirituality and Loving Relationship. This instrument can be accessed from the

ChurchSmart resources in Illinois, or from the Center for Leadership in Winfield British Columbia.

The Precept group is a church marketing company that helps churches to gather important demographic and psychograpic information relevant to their ministry context. Percept is one of the leading information providers to religious organizations for the past 14 years. Percept currently serves over 240 denominational regional bodies and national offices from all across the United States. Percept provides a blend of demographic and ethnographic information that is able to combine the benefit of technology, the latest statistical analysis, and surveys of the congregation to help a church more effectively accomplish its mission.

Through Percept a congregation can evaluate the context of its mission field and better plan for future ministry. The rapid changes that are happening around us make it imperative for congregations to know as much as they can in order to be more effective in ministry. Percept helps congregations to do just that. For a fee this group will also administer a church assessment that will help the church reposition itself to do effective ministry. Churches interested in getting more information about Precept can contact http://www.link2lead.com.

Community Assessment

One of the critical factors in ministering effectively to any community is knowing the community. George Barna in his book *Church Marketing: Breaking Ground for the Harvest,* underscores the importance of knowing one's context for effective ministry. He notes, "history shows that all good decisions are made within a realistic understanding of the decision-making environment. If you want to understand God's vision for your church, get a grip on the details of your ministry environment (1992:127). Gathering community data is an attempt to understand this context.

The kinds of data a church will need to gather about the community are the following. What are the top needs this community faces? When a church seeks to minister where people's needs are it has no choice but to grow. Growth becomes a by product of doing the right things. Another question that must be asked is what are the recurring problems in this community? When problems are recurring in a community, there is a certain frustration level that also builds within that community. Added to this there will also be an openness on the part of the community to seek some group or groups to help make a difference. This is where the church comes in. Partnerships can be fostered because of such openness.

Another critical question that must be asked is what resources are available to meet these needs? If the needs in the community are already being met it makes no sense for a church to duplicate the services. Do something that no one else is doing. Finally, a church must ask how can we make a difference? This question must be answered in two ways. Are the needs in the community ones we can meet by ourselves? Or do we need to partner with other groups in the community? Community partnership plays an essential role in network evangelism. Such partnerships create a perception in the community that a church is not just concern about spiritual matters.

Some of the areas from which data can be collected are the Police Department, Community Health, Safe Shelters, Department of Social Services and the schools. These are the institutions that have a handle on the heart beat of the community. They will tell a church what are the key needs in the community. Such data can be collected through demographic surveys, interviews or community awareness evenings.

Community awareness evenings are times that a church sets aside where community leaders are brought in to share, from their departments' perspectives, what the critical needs in community might be.

Developing a Clear Strategy

The next step in starting an assimilation ministry in a church is to develop a clear ministry strategy based on the strength of the church and the critical needs in the community. It will be important to prioritize the top two needs that a church can address. These needs should be formalized into what can be called pre-evangelistic ministries. A church should not try to do too many such ministries, but two are three are good. Key is understanding that these pre-evangelistic ministries are designed to reach into the needs of the community and bridge people to Christ and his

Church. Once these events or ministries are planned, strategic considerations must be given to the rails that will be developed to help people connect to Christ and His Church. In pre - evangelistic ministries, it is important to build relationships with people. Also it is critical to help the community see what the church is about. This can be done through posters, information tables with brochures, or multimedia presentations.

The next stage of the strategy is to sure up "first impression" ministries. To do this ushers and greeters must be trained to understand their ministries as evangelistic. They should see their ministries as ministering to the stranger. Their role is to help new persons feel comfortable as they attend church. A church must also decide other forms of "first impression ministries" such as follow up letters, phone calls, visitation etc.

An important aspect of firming up "first impression" ministries is determining the necessary information that a church needs to gather on attenders. This data will help in the follow-up process. Here is a list of the records a church needs to keep, if it is going to do effective assimilation. It is necessary to keep a list of first time attenders. This can be done through filling out, something like a friendship and communication's card during the service. One note about this, all the people should fill this out, not just the visitors. This normalizes the process and does not allow visitors to feel conspicuous. A record of those visitors who are returning and becoming regular attenders should also be kept. Conversion records are also necessary. The number of people who are no longer attending the church and the reason for their not attending should also be kept.

If a church wants to see if it is growing through conversion or transfer, it should know how people become a part of the church. Therefore a category must be developed on how people become members of the church. Other records that are helpful in determining assimilation are average attendance, number of people who are inactive and number of people involved in ministry. These records can be kept in an assimilation data base. The next chapter will introduce some assimilation software that are designed to do all that has been discussed plus more.

The next part of the assimilation strategy has to do with helping people to become Christians, discipled to maturity, and released to serve according to their ministry profiles. Every church must develop a clear discipleship path for people. This is the surest way to close the back door of a church. When people understand what it means to be a Christian, what their gifts and passions are for ministry, and are ministering accordingly, then they are more satisfied and fulfilled in ministry. They will want to invest their time and talents in building God's kingdom through the local church.

The final aspect of the strategy is to sure up your back door. Allusions have already been made to this in the previous chapter. A church must decide how it will reach out to people who are dissatisfied with the church for one reason or another and want to leave. It is important for the church to attempt to restore such people. A formalized process must be set in place. Public reputation is critical for any volunteer organization, including the church. Therefore when a person leaves a church, it is best if that person can leave with a good report. Sometimes this is not possible but the church should seek to err on the side of grace - trying to reach out to them in the best possible way.

Key Concepts

Conversion Growth: This is when people are added to the church because they have become Christians.

Transfer Growth: This is when persons are added to the church because they are transferring their membership from another church, whether formally or informally.

Inactive Members: Inactive members are people who attend church sporadically. They are not involved in any particular ministry or small group.

Means of Member Addition: This refers to the way new people are added to the church. Did they come through conversion or transfer? Did a friend invite them to church? Was it because of a family member? Was it because the church has a good reputation in the community and therefore that reputation draws people? It is helpful to have this information. If a church knows the primary ways people are added to it, it can choose to maximize such doors. In some cases it might choose to change strategies to a more preferred means of addition such as conversion as against transfer.

For Reflection and Action

1. Do a five year assessment of your church and determine your yearly, attendance average, drop out rate and means of new member addition.
2. How would you characterize your church; growing, declining or plateau?
3. Based on your characterization why do you believe your church is where it is currently?
4. How open is your church to forming community partnerships in order to do ministry?

A Guide to Assimilation in the Local Church

Have you made peace with technology?

CHAPTER 9

ASSIMILATION AND THE TECHNOLOGICAL REVOLUTION

Today the Church faces many challenges. Secularism is rampant. Pluralism is the order of the day. Relativism is challenging the nature of the gospel it preaches. Church attendance is declining. Evangelism is taking a back seat in most churches. Many churches have not even keyed into the need to do effective assimilation. Maybe more accurately some churches do not even know what assimilation is really about. Added to all those changes a major technological revolution is taking place.

The revolution in electronic technology has changed the way we communicate. Fax machines, high speed modems, and Internet access have made communication more accessible. For example, no longer is a face to face gathering the only effective way to conduct meetings. It is possible to have meetings through video conferencing. These changes raise the expectations of parishioners within the church. Many do not care much for meetings. The Church has to find new ways of conducting its business. The technological revolution, however leaves many people even more desirous of relationships. In many ways technology decreases personal touch. Sharing the gospel in a technological society has to capitalize on the need for relationships and personal touch. It is precisely at this point that the church can design pre-evangelistic ministries that help people to build relationships. Need based small groups is a good method to accomplish that end. Churches are being called upon to embrace technology and use it to make ministry more effective. Unfortunately some churches still have not made friend with technology. Therefore they are using old tools to do ministry in a technological age. The result is frustration and stagnation. Frustration sets in because pastors and leaders cannot seem to understand why they are working so hard with so little result. The truth is, they are using the wrong tools. It is not working harder but smarter. Growth in the age of post-modernity requires the embracing of languages and forms that communicate to a post-modern culture. When this does not happen a church that is caught in a time warp does not grow. It stagnates and soon declines.

The following section will introduce several church management and growth software, that with proper customization, can help a church with assimilation. These softwares are designed to move churches into the technological age. The key ones that will be introduced are: The Shelby Systems, Church Management and, Servant Keeper. I do not claim to be an authority on any of them, but having worked with assimilation ministry over the years I have come to see how these softwares can be customized to aid with assimilation.

Over View of Some Church Management Software

The Shelby System is one of the oldest church management software that is available today. It has been around since 1976. This software has gone through many revisions and evolutions. The product can be accessed at www.shelbyinc.com. It is very comprehensive, but customizable for assimilation need. Among its many features are attendance tracking, contributions positing and reporting, membership and prospects management among many others.

In the attendance module the Shelby Systems will allow you to develop class rosters; customized to your specific needs; show attendance history, allow you to enter data by name, name ID or class roster. It will allow you to store and retrieve attendance history of up to five years. The system allows you to analyze data according to trends, seasonal patterns and specific campaigns or events results.

The prospect features allow you to keep the kind of information that will enable your church to communicate with potential members. In it you can manage small groups, membership, meeting times and overall attendance. Many medium size churches struggle to develop and maintain a proper church scheduling program. Consequently members are prone to enter into repeated conflicts because of the desire to use the same space for activities. The Shelby Systems allows you to develop a proper scheduling program where all events can be properly scheduled and the appropriate rooms booked. In this way the possibility of conflict over the use of space is minimized. The only real draw back for the Shelby System is the price.

A church will have to invest a considerable amount of money in order to access its best features. Nevertheless it is a good assimilation software.

Greentree Applied Church Management System is also another that can be recommended. It is much less expensive than the Shelby System but does much the same. Among its features are complete membership information, quick- find browsing capabilities, contributions accounting reporting, complete visitor information, complete audit trail, general ledgering, personal profiles, spiritual gifts and talent tracking, ministries attendance tracking, multi-level password protection among others.

One of the unique features of this program is that it will allow you easy data conversion if you were already using another church management software. A small fee is required for the conversion. As a church grows its health depends on the church's ability to keep in touch with its members, visitors and prospects.

This software will help you to do that. To preview this software one can go to www.Churchmembershipsoftware.com

Servant Keeper is among the best church management softwares available today. It is very user friendly. Once personal information is entered into the program it automatically moves this information to all the appropriate areas in the program where this information will be needed. With just a click of the mouse you are able to add new fields. It is very customizable. If a church is already using a previous church management system the Servant Keeper support line will also help you convert your data from that system to Servant Keeper, for a minimal fee. Standard in this software are all the regular features that most church management systems would have such as membership, individual and family profile, attendance and contribution. Some of the features it has that some church management systems do not have are pictorial directory, links to Quicken and Quick books and also links to phone tree. Both Quicken and Quick books are accounting programs. It is a helpful feature to have your contribution data directly interfacing with your accounting program. Phone Tree is an automatic phone dialing system that allows a church to communicate with its members through auto - dialing. This saves many hours of human time. Servant Keeper is priced mid ranged. It can be accessed from www.servantkeeper.com.

When choosing any computer software for your church you should be guided by a few considerations. First is it customizable enough to meet my needs? This is an important question, since all of these church management softwares tend to have a customer support line. However it is only so much help they will allow before you will have to start paying for it, or you become so frustrated that you stop calling. Many of them assume a certain level of database knowledge.

Therefore the kind of help they will give might not be as basic as some churches need. A church must make a decision to keep somebody in house adequately trained to be able to customize the software sufficiently with limited use of the technical support lines.

A second question has to do with usage. If the software is widely used then there is a good chance that enough is being said about it that can be accessed. It is the responsibility of all purchasers to adequately research the product to see if it is as good as the producers say it is. Also the wider the usage the more accountable the producers will be, since it is likely that they would have received much feedback on the product. Such feed back should improve the product.

A third question is afford-ability. Not all small churches can afford to designate five or six thousand dollars for a program. Therefore cost must be a factor. One of the ways to determine how much should be spent for a product is to first determine exactly what is needed. Many of these church management systems are produced on various levels. Some are for small churches, medium size churches and large churches. If your church is small buy a small version and as your church grows adjust accordingly.

Recommended Customization

The following are some recommended customization that are necessary to be made in any software if a church will do effectively assimilation. Fields must be created that will determine the number of people involved in ministry, small groups, and both small groups and ministries. This is not very difficult since, if the proper customization is done queries could just be set to generate the above custom reports. A church should also be able to sort information by any age group required. This means if you need to know how many adults are involved in ministry you should be able to establish a query to grant that information.

Fields should also be set to determine inactive people, people who attend church sporadically, people who have moved, quit, died, transferred to another church etc. It is also necessary to sort people by the number of first time visitors a church had any particular year, people who were added to the church through conversion, transfer or any other means. All these programs will allow you to add any number of fields necessary to produce the kind of statistics that might be necessary.

If the above customizations are done then each year, a church should be able to measure its performance by generating such reports as the percentage of first time visitors it assimilates, the number of people who are integrated in the church by involvement in small groups and the amount of people who are lost from the church in any given year.

Some churches might be afraid of keeping such objective data. But it is for that very reason that those churches will not be able to measure their growth. A lack of objective data only allows those churches to assume that they are growing. Such assumptions might be wrong but they do not know. The bible tells us those who win souls are wise. Wisdom would dictate that churches need to measure how they are doing. If they are not doing well they now have the opportunity to change and do better. The process of assimilation outlined in this guide should move a church to a more objective form of doing ministry.

Calculating Assimilation

Assimilation is calculated in two ways. First a church should determine the number of first time visitors who are becoming regular attenders to the church each year. This is called new member assimilation. An example would be, if a church records three hundred first time visitors a particular year and one hundred and fifty of those people become regular attenders. Then the church has a newcomer assimilation rate of fifty percent. This should help the church to improve its first impression ministries. It is important to note that a church will not be able to assimilate all the visitors who attend church a particular year. Sometimes visitors are from outside the city and are only at church because they are visiting a family member. Other times people might be from other churches but are attending a special function held at your church. It is therefore necessary to set up fields in the software to filter out people who are not realistic prospects for assimilation.

The second form of assimilation that should be calculated is membership involvement. This applies to the entire church. A reasonable standard is to consider persons assimilated when they are involved in at least one ministry and one small group. For children or youth a standard would be when they have moved from a fishing pool activity to a regular growth opportunity in the church. These regular growth opportunities could be Sunday schools, bible studies or even small groups.

Fishing pool activities are event oriented. It takes less commitment to attend such activities. A regular growth opportunity requires a different kind of commitment. Usually when people make a commitment to a regular growth opportunity they are making a statement about the kind of commitment they are making. It must be remembered that assimilation is a process, consequently the goal is to help people move through the various stages until they become fully functioning parts of the body of Christ.

Key Concepts

Church Management Software: This is any computer program that allows a church to establish a database for tracking membership, developing and recording member profiles, and integrating a number of church management procedures.

Calculating Assimilation: Assimilation should be calculated from two perspectives: new member and existing members. New member assimilation refers to the total number of visitors a church has been able to retain over a given year. This is done by calculating the percentage of visitors kept, times one hundred divided by the total number of visitors for that year. Existing member assimilation refers to the rate at which existing members becomeg fully engaged into the church life. Each church might need to set a standard for this, e.g. when members are involved in one ministry and a small group. This calculation is done by multiplying the total number of persons who have reached the established standard, times one hundred divided by the total membership of the church.

For Reflection and Action

1. What church management system does your church currently use?
2. If it is not using one what is the biggest obstacle that your church face in selecting a proper church management software?
3. Do you know the number of first time visitors who attend your church yearly? How many of them has your church been able to retain?
4. How many of your current members are fully assimilated into the body of Christ? What standard have you set to determine member assimilation?

CONCLUSION

My prayer in writing this guide, is that all churches, both small and large would rise to the challenge of rethinking the way they evangelize and assimilate people into the life the church. The church preaches a gospel of love. It is important that when new people attend churches they experience that love. It is even better if they experience that love before they attend church. That would give evidence of God's people being at work in His world.

The mandate of Christ is clear "all authority in heaven and on earth has been given to me. Therefore go and make disciples of all nations, baptizing them in the name of the Father and of the Son and the Holy Spirit, and teaching them to obey everything I have commanded you. And surely I am with you always, to the very end of the age" (Matt. 28-18-20). These were the words of Christ. Evangelizing and discipling people are foundational to the mission of the Church. If this is so the Church has to continue to listen to God to find fresh, new ways to share the message of the gospel.

In the introduction mention was made, that the Church must be a careful student of culture and also of the scriptures, in order to be effective. The danger is to do one without the other. It is possible to seek to be faithful in studying and teaching the bible to the exclusion of understanding our culture. The result of this practice is spiritual elitism. Non-Christians are not attracted to spiritual elitism. The other extreme is equally dangerous. It is possible to be so sociological and anthropological, seeking to understand the culture, and fail to hear God a fresh through the scriptures. This assimilation guide asks the church to strike a balance. Study the culture in order to be relevant. Study the scriptures in order to disciple more effectively. When both the scriptures and the culture are brought together then mission can happen. People become sensitized to the needs around them and are motivated by the scriptures to seek to make a difference. My prayer is that this simple guide will move churches towards truly becoming relevant, biblical and mission driven.

A Guide to Assimilation in the Local Church

APPENDIX

Sample of First Time Visitor Letter

Dear:

We are so happy that you chose to worship with us last Sunday. We hope that you felt right at home in our service and that you received a word of encouragement and inspiration that strengthened your life.

If you do not presently attend a church, we would be delighted for you to become a part of the family at the(your church). We invite you to come share in the worship and fellowship on a regular basis.

The (your church)cares a great deal about each person who attends. We offer a variety of programs and ministries that are especially designed to meet the needs of those in the church and community.

If you have any questions about the (church's name), its beliefs, programs or ministry opportunities, do not hesitate to call me or others of our pastoral staff. We want to help you in any way we can.

Sincerely,

(Senior Pastor's Name)
Senior Pastor

Missing in Attendance Letters

(Person missing three weeks in a row)

Dear

At (your church's name) we value the fellowship of friends. In fact, when one person is missing, worship is not the same. It is our sincere desire to provide the best possible care for our congregants. So it is in that context of ministry and care that we write this letter.

We have missed you worshiping with us for the past three weeks. We just want you to know that we are praying for you. If there is anything that we can do for you please don't hesitate to call.

God's Blessings,

Pastor's name

A Guide to Assimilation in the Local Church

Person missing five weeks in a row

Dear:

For the past several weeks I have missed you worshiping with us at church. I hope everything is going fine for you.

I look forward to seeing you worship with us this Sunday. In the meantime, if I can be of assistance to you, please do not hesitate to call me at (church's number).

I want you to know that I will be praying especially for you this week.

See you Sunday.

Pastor's name

Person did not return after visiting for the first time

Dear:

I missed seeing you this week! Please give me a call if I can be of assistance or answer questions you may have about the church or its ministries.

God bless

Pastor's name

A Guide to Assimilation in the Local Church

Follow - up Letter

Dear:

I missed you last Sunday! Give me a call if I can assist you in any way. I do care about and pray for each of our attenders.

God bless,

Pastor's name

If the Person Attends Sporadically

Dear:

I am very happy that you have chosen to visit with us again. Your presence with us has been missed. I look forward to your worshiping with us on a more regular basis.

I hope your worship experience was very meaningful last Sunday. My prayer is that God will continue to be good to you.

Sincerely,

Pastor's name

Sample 2 - Sporadic Letter

Dear:

Your presence with us has been missed for the last while. I am very happy that you have chosen to visit with us again. I look forward to you worshiping with us on a more regular basis.

I hope your worship experience was very meaningful on Sunday morning. If there is anything that I can do for you, please call the church and we can set up a time that would be suitable for us to meet together. My prayer is that God will continue to be good to you.

Sincerely,

Pastor's name

Letters for Special Occasion

If the Person is on Holidays

Dear,

Several weeks have passed since we last saw you at church. We know that this is your holiday time. We hope that your holidays will bring personal refreshment and renewal to you.
We want you to know that you are loved and missed. We are praying that all will go well for you. We look forward to seeing you soon.

God bless!

Pastor's name

If the Person is Sick

Dear,

We realize that you are recuperating from major surgery. It is so important for you to take this time to allow your body to mend. I am praying that God will continue to give you renewed strength and encouragement to meet each day.

If I can be of any assistance to you during this time, please feel free to call me.

I want you to know that you are loved and missed at (church's name). We all look forward to seeing you soon.

God bless!

Pastor's name

Person visiting Because of a Baptism - Sample 1

Dear,

Sunday was a very special day in the lives of many people. It was a special day of worship celebration. We consider ourselves very privileged to have had you share that special time with us.

We know many of you came to see your relatives and friends get baptized. Thank you so much for coming. We trust that you felt the presence of God richly in your lives as you worshiped with us.

Baptism is always a special time of celebration for God's church, and we say God's church because God only has one church. Baptism is a time when people publicly declare their desire to follow the Lord. It is also a time to publicly declare our new identity in Christ. Thanks for making that special moment even more special for your loved ones, friends and all of us.

We would love to have you visiting with us again in the near future. May God's blessings be yours.

See you soon.
Pastor's name

Owen Facey

Person Visiting Because of a Baptism - Sample 2

Dear,

Sunday was a very special day in the lives of many people. Being Easter Sunday, it was a special day of worship celebration. We consider ourselves very privileged to have had you share that special time with us.

We know many of you came to see your relatives and friends get baptized. Thank you so much for coming. We trust that you felt the presence of God richly in your lives as you worshiped with us.

Baptism is always a special time of celebration for God's church, and we say God's church because God only has one church. Baptism is a time when people publicly declare their desire to follow the Lord. It is also a time to publicly declare our new identity in Christ. Thanks for making that special moment even more special for your loved ones, friends and all of us.

We would love to have you visiting with us again in the near future. May God's blessings be yours.

See you soon.

Pastor's name

Person Visiting Because of Christmas Holidays

Dear,

Thank you for worshiping with us last Sunday. We realize that you were in the area spending Christmas with family and friends. What a wonderful time of year when we celebrate Christ's birth.

We hope the service was very meaningful to you. We also hope you were able to enjoy the presence of God. We invite you to drop in again whenever you are in town.

May the blessings of God be yours in the New Year.

Sincerely,

(Pastor's Name)
Senior Pastor

A Guide to Assimilation in the Local Church

Person Visiting Because of a Friend Day Celebration

Dear,

Sunday was a special day in the house of the Lord. It was Friend Day. The day was even more special because you chose to worship with us. From the staff and church community at (Church name) we are expressing our heartfelt thanks to you for choosing to worship with us. We hope that as you worshiped you felt the presence of God.

It is our desire to serve each person who comes through the church's doors the best possible way. We would suggest that if you do not have a church home where you worship regularly we would be happy to have you worshiping with us. Also, if you have any questions or concerns, or if we could be of any help to you please don't hesitate to call us at (phone number)

Again, thank you so much for being our friend on Friend Day.

We look forward to seeing you again soon.

Your Friend,
Pastor's name

Father's Day Celebration

Dear,

Sunday was a special day in the house of the Lord. It was Father's Day. A day when families come together to pay tribute to that special person in their lives. From the staff and church community at (church's name) we are expressing our heartfelt thanks to you for choosing to worship with us. We hope that as you worshiped you felt the presence of God.

We hope the service was very meaningful to you. We also hope you were able to enjoy the presence of God. We invite you to drop in again whenever you are in town.

We look forward to seeing you again soon.

Sincerely,

Pastor's name

A Guide to Assimilation in the Local Church

Mother's Day Celebration

Dear,

Sunday was a special day in the house of the Lord. It was Mother's Day. A day when families come together to pay tribute to that special person in their lives. From the staff and church community at (your church's name) we are expressing our heartfelt thanks to you for choosing to worship with us. We hope that as you worshiped you felt the presence of God.

It is our desire to serve each person who comes through the church's doors the best possible way. We would suggest that if you do not have a church home where you worship regularly we would be happy to have you worshiping with us. Also, if you have any questions or concerns, or if we could be of any help to you please don't hesitate to call us at church's number.

We look forward to seeing you again soon.

Sincerely,

Pastor's name

Person Visiting From Out of The City

(They might not be a legitimate prospect for your church)

Dear,

Your presence in our worship service last Sunday added much to its dynamic and richness. Thank you for choosing the (church's name)to be your place of worship.

We hope the service was very meaningful to you. We also hope you were able to enjoy the presence of God. We invite you to drop in again whenever you are in town.

May the blessings of God be yours.

Sincerely,

Pastor's name

Senior Pastor

A Guide to Assimilation in the Local Church

Person Visiting Because of Parent Child Dedication

Dear,

Sunday was a special day in the house of the Lord. It was Parent/Child Dedication. A day when families come together to support the parents of a child to be dedicated to the Lord.. From the staff and church community at (church's name) we are expressing our heartfelt thanks to you for choosing to worship with us. We hope that as you worshiped you felt the presence of God.

It is our desire to serve each person who comes through the church's doors the best possible way. We would suggest that if you do not have a church home where you worship regularly we would be happy to have you worshiping with us. Also, if you have any questions or concerns, or if we could be of any help to you please don't hesitate to call us at (church's number).

We look forward to seeing you again soon.

Sincerely,

Pastor's name

WORKS CITED

Barna, George
1992 *Church Marketing, Breaking Ground for the Harvest*. Ventura, CA: Regal Books.
1996 *Moving From Vision to Action*. Ventura, CA: Regal Books.

Bast, Robert
1988 *Attracting New Members*. Monrovia, CA: Church Growth Inc.

Beasley-Murray, George R.
1987 *Word Biblical Commentary, St. John.* Dallas, TX: Word Books Publishers.

Bibby, Reginald
1995 *There's Got to Be More*. Winfield, BC: Wood Lake Books Inc.

Bugbee, Burce
1995 *What You do Best In the Body of Christ*. Gand Rapids, MI: Zondervan Publishing House

Depree, Max
1989 *Leadership is an Art*. New York, NY: Dell Trade Publishing.

Glenn, Sylvia
n.d. *Assimilation . . . Helping People Become a Part of the Family*. Anderson, Indiana: The

Board of Church Extension and Home Missions of The Church of God Anderson Indiana.

Green, Michael
1990 *Evangelism in the Early Church.* Surrey, UK: Inter Publishing Service

Hunter, George
1996 *A Church for the Unchurched.* Nashville, TN. Abingdon Press.

Kalestad, Walt and Steve Shey
1994 *Total Quality Ministry.* Minneapolis, MN: Augsburg Fortress.

Kouzes, James and Barry Posner
1995 *The Leadership Challenge: How to Keep Getting Extraordinary Things Done in Organizations.* San Francisco, CA: Jossey-Bass Publishers.

Littauer, Florence
1984 *How To Get Along With Difficult People.* Eugene, OR: Harvest House Publishers.

Logan, Robert and Larry Short
1994 *Mobilizing for Compassion, Moving People into Ministry.* Grand Rapids, MI: Fleming H. Revell

Packer, J. I

1966 *Evangelism and the Sovereignty of God.* London: Inter-Varsity Fellowship

Peters, Tom
1994 *The Tom Peters Seminar, Crazy Times Call for Crazy Organizations.* Toronto, ON: Random House.

Quinn, Robert E.
1996 *Deep Change, Discovering the Leader Within You.* San Francisco, CA: Jossey-Bass Publishers

Salter, Dairus
1996 *American Evangelism Its Theology and Practise.* Grand Rapids, MI: Baker Book House Company.

Sanders, James
1984 *Canon and Community: A Guide to Canonical Criticism.* Philadelphia, PA: Fortress Press.

Slocum, Robert
1993 *Maximize Your Ministry.* Colorado Springs, CO: NavPress.

Withrow, Oral
1991 *Your Church Can Grow.* Anderson, IN: Warner Press.

About The Author

Owen Facey is a graduate of Anderson University, School of theology, from which he receives the Master of Divinity degree. He also holds a Doctor of Ministry degree from Fuller Theological Seminary. He has been pastoring for the past sixteen years. During that period of time he has served in various capacities, as Minister of Evangelism and Discipleship, Minister of Assimilation and Church growth and pastor. Owen is currently serving as pastor at the Church of God of West Broward, Plantation Fl. He is also a church consultant and seminar leader.

Printed in the United States
16823LVS00001B/124